SEVENTY-EIGHT
DEGREES OF
WISDOM

A psychological approach to the Tarot, examining all
aspects of the cards – their origins, symbolism and their
historical, mythological and esoteric background.

By the same author
SEVENTY-EIGHT DEGREES OF WISDOM
    PART 2: The Minor Arcana
TAROT: THE OPEN LABYRINTH

SEVENTY-EIGHT DEGREES OF WISDOM

A BOOK OF TAROT

Part I: The Major Arcana

Rachel Pollack

THE AQUARIAN PRESS LIMITED
Wellingborough, Northamptonshire

First published 1980
Second Impression April 1984
Third Impression November 1984
Fourth Impression July 1985
Fifth Impression May 1986

ISBN 0 85030 220 X

Printed and bound in Great Britain

Contents

To Marilyn, who taught me so much by becoming my student. And to Edie, the best reader I know.

Introduction

Origins of the Tarot

 round the middle of the fifteenth century, not so long after the first written references in Europe to cards of any kind, an artist named Bonifacio Bembo painted a set of unnamed and unnumbered cards for the Visconti family of Milan. These pictures comprise the classic deck for an Italian game called 'Tarocchi': four suits of fourteen cards each, plus twenty-two cards showing different scenes and later called 'triomffi' – in English, 'triumphs', or 'trumps'.

Now, of these twenty-two images many can be interpreted as simply a catalogue of medieval social types, such as (to give them their later names) 'the Pope' or 'the Emperor', or else common medieval moral homilies, such as 'the Wheel of Fortune'. Some represent virtues, like 'Temperance' or 'Fortitude'. Others show religious-mythological scenes, such as the dead rising from the grave at the trumpet call for 'the Last Judgement'. There is even a card depicting a popular heresy, the image of a female pope, which we can describe as a joke on the Church with rather deeper significance than most ecclesiastical humour. Still, we can view this heretical picture as deeply rooted in popular culture, and therefore obvious to someone representing medieval 'types'.

One figure, however, stands out as rather strange. It shows a young man hanging upside down by his left leg from a simple wooden frame. His hands are held casually behind his back to form a triangle with his head at the bottom, his right leg is bent behind his knee to produce the figure of a cross, or else the numeral four. The face appears relaxed, even perhaps entranced. Where did Bembo derive this image? It certainly does not represent a criminal hanged at the gallows, as some later artists have assumed.

Christian tradition describes St Peter as being crucified upside down, ostensibly so he could not be said to be copying his Lord. In the Elder Edda, however, the god Odin is described as hanging upside down from the World Tree for nine days and nights, not as a punishment, but in order to receive enlightenment, the gift of prophecy. But this mythological scene itself derives from the actual practice of shamans, medicine men and women, in such places as Siberia and North America. In the initiation and training the candidates for shamanism are sometimes told to hang upside down in precisely the manner shown in Bembo's card. Apparently the reversal of the body produces some sort of psychological benefit, in the way that starvation and extreme cold will induce radiant visions. The alchemists – who, with the witches, were possibly the survivors of the shamanist tradition in Europe – also hung themselves upside down, believing that elements in the sperm vital to immortality would thus flow down to the psychic centres at the top of the head. And even before the West began to take Yoga seriously everyone knew the image of the yogi standing on his head.

Did Bembo simply wish to represent an alchemist? Then why not use the more common image, that of a bearded man stirring a cauldron or mixing chemicals? The picture, titled 'the Hanged Man' in subsequent decks and later made famous by T.S. Eliot in *The Wasteland*, appears not so much as an alchemist as a young initiate in some secret tradition. Was Bembo himself an initiate? The special crossing of the legs, an esoteric sign from secret societies, would suggest so. And if he included one reference to esoteric practices, might not other images, superficially a social commentary, in reality represent an entire body of occult knowledge? Why, for instance, did the original deck contain twenty-two cards, not say, twenty or twenty-one or twenty-five, all of which are more commonly given significance in Western culture? Was it chance, or did Bembo (or perhaps others whom Bembo simply copied) wish to slyly represent the esoteric meanings connected to the twenty-two letters of the Hebrew alphabet? And yet, if any evidence exists anywhere connecting Bembo or the Visconti family to any occult group no one has produced it for public scrutiny.

A brief look at the stunning correspondences between the Tarot and the body of Jewish mysticism and occult knowledge, called collectively the Qabalah, will demonstrate the way in which Bembo's cards seem almost to demand an esoteric interpretation, despite the lack of hard evidence. The Qabalah dwells very deeply on the symbolism of the Hebrew alphabet. The letters are connected to the paths of the Tree of Life and they are each given their own symbolic meanings. Now, the Hebrew alphabet contains, as noted, twenty-two letters, the same number as the trumps of Tarocchi. The Qabalah also goes deeply into the four letters of God's unpronounceable name, YHVH. They represent the four worlds of creation, the four basic elements of medieval science, four stages of existence, four methods of interpreting the Bible, and so on. There are four court cards in each of Bembo's four suits.

Finally, the Qabalah works with the number ten – the Ten Commandments and ten sephiroth (stages of emanation) on each of the four Trees of Life. And the four suits contain cards numbered from one to ten. Do we wonder then that Tarot commentators have claimed that the deck originated as a pictorial version of the Qabalah, meaningless to the masses, but highly potent to the few? And yet, in all the thousands of pages of Qabalistic literature, not one word appears about the Tarot.

Occultists have claimed secret sources for the cards, such as a grand conference of Qabalists and other Masters in Morocco in 1300, but no one has ever produced any historical evidence for such claims. Even more damning, Tarot commentators themselves do not mention the Qabalah until the nineteenth century. And of course, the names and numbers sequence, so vital to their interpretations, came after the original images.

If we accept Carl Jung's idea of basic spiritual archetypes structured into the human mind we can perhaps say that Bembo unconsciously tapped hidden springs of knowledge, allowing later imaginations to make the conscious connections. And yet, such exact and complete correspondences as the twenty-two trumps, the four court cards and ten pip cards in the four suits, or the position and ecstatic face of the Hanged Man, would seem to strain even such a potent force as the Collective Unconscious.

For years Tarocchi was seen primarily as a game for gambling, and to a much lesser extent as a device for fortune-telling. Then, in the eighteenth century, an occultist named Antoine Court de Gebelin declared the Tarot (as the French called the game) to be the remnant of the Book of Thoth, created by the Egyptian god of magic to convey all knowledge to his disciples. Court de Gebelin's idea appears far more fanciful than factual, but in the nineteenth century another Frenchman, Alphonse Louis Constant, known as Eliphas Lévi, linked the cards to the Qabalah, and since then people have looked deeper and deeper into the Tarot, finding more and more meanings, wisdom, and even, through meditation and deep study, enlightenment.

Today, we see the Tarot as a kind of path, a way to personal growth through understanding of ourselves and life. To some the Tarot's origin remains a vital question; for others it only matters that meanings have accrued to the cards over the years.

For Bembo did create an archetype, whether consciously or from deep instinct. Beyond any system or detailed explanations, the images themselves, changed and elaborated over the years by different artists, fascinate and entrance us. In this way they draw us into their mysterious world which ultimately can never be explained, but only experienced.

Different Versions of the Tarot

Most modern Tarots differ very little from those fifteenth century sets of cards. They still contain seventy-eight cards divided into the four suits, Wands, Cups, Swords, and Coins or Pentacles, called collectively the 'Minor Arcana', and the twenty-two trumps, known as the 'Major Arcana' (the word 'arcanum' means 'secret knowledge'). True, some of the pictures have changed considerably, but each version usually keeps the same basic concept. For example, there are several widely varying versions of the Emperor, but they all represent some idea of an Emperor. In general, the changes have tended towards the more symbolic and the more mystical.

This book uses as its primary source, the Tarot of Arthur Edward Waite, whose very popular Rider pack (named after its British publisher) appeared in 1910. Waite was criticized for changing some of the trump cards from their accepted version. For instance, the common picture of the Sun shows two children holding hands in a garden. Waite changed it to one child on a horse riding *out* of a garden. The critics claimed Waite was altering the card's meaning to his personal vision. This was probably the case, since Waite believed more strongly in his own ideas than those of anyone else. But few people stopped to consider that the earliest version of the Sun, that of Bembo, in no way resembles the supposed 'traditional' version. Indeed, it seems closer to Waite's; the picture shows a single miraculous child flying through the air, holding up a globe with an image of a city inside it.

The most striking change Waite and his artist, Pamela Colman Smith, made was to include a scene on all the cards, including the numbered cards of the Minor Arcana. Virtually all previous decks, as well as many later ones, have simple geometric patterns for the 'pip' cards. For example, the ten of Swords will show ten swords arranged in a pattern, much like its descendant, the ten of spades. The Rider pack is different. Pamela Smith's ten of Swords shows a man lying under a black cloud with ten swords stuck in his back and legs.

We do not really know who actually designed these cards. Did Waite himself conceive them (as he undoubtedly did the Major Arcana), or did he simply tell Smith the qualities and ideas he wanted and allow her to invent the scenes? Waite's own book on the Tarot, *The Pictorial Key to the Tarot*, makes little real use of the pictures. In some cases, such as the six of Swords, the picture suggests far more than Waite's stated meaning, while in others, particularly the two of Swords, the picture almost contradicts the meaning.

Whether it was Waite or Smith who designed the pictures, they had a powerful effect on later Tarot designers. Almost all decks with scenes on every card rely very heavily on the pictures in the Rider pack.

Waite called his deck the 'rectified Tarot'. He insisted that his pictures 'restored' the true meanings of the cards, and throughout his book he scorns the versions of his predecessors. Now, by 'rectified' many people will think Waite's membership in secret societies gave him access to the 'original' secret Tarot. More likely, he simply meant that his pictures gave the cards their deepest meanings. When he so drastically altered the card of the Lovers, for instance, he did so because he thought the old picture insignificant and his new one symbolic of a deep truth.

I do not mean to suggest that Waite's cards are simply an intellectual construction, like a scholar rearranging some speech of Hamlet's in a way which makes more sense to him. Waite was a mystic, an occultist, and a student of magic and esoteric practices. He based his Tarot on deep personal experience of enlightenment. He believed his Tarot to be right and the others wrong because it represented that experience.

I have chosen the Rider pack as my source for two reasons. Firstly, I find many of its innovations extremely valuable. The Waite-Smith version of the Fool strikes me as more meaningful than any of the earlier ones. Secondly, the revolutionary change in the Minor Arcana seems to me to free us from the formulas that dominated the suit cards for so long. Previously, once you read and memorized the given meanings of a Minor card you could not really add to it; the picture suggested very little. In the Rider pack we can allow the picture to work on the subconscious; we can also apply our own experience to it. In short, Pamela Smith has given us something to interpret.

Above I wrote that I chose the Rider pack as my 'primary' source. Most books on the Tarot use one deck alone for illustrations. This self-limitation perhaps stems from a desire to represent the 'true' Tarot. By choosing one deck and not another we are really declaring that one is correct and the other is false. Such a declaration matters most to those writers, like Aleister Crowley or Paul Foster Case, who consider the Tarot a symbolic system of objective knowledge. This book, however, looks upon the cards more as an archetype of experience. Seen that way no deck is right or wrong, but is simply a furthering of the archetype. The Tarot is both the total of all the different versions over the years, and an entity apart from any of them. In the cases where a version other than Waite's will deepen the meaning of a specific card we will look at both images. In some cases, Judgement for instance, or the Moon, the differences are subtle; in others, the Lovers, or the Fool, the difference is drastic. By looking at several versions of the same experience we heighten our awareness of that experience.

Divination

Today, most people see the Tarot as a means of fortune-telling, or 'divination'. Strangely, we know less historically about this aspect of the cards than any other. Judging by the comparatively few historical references to divination as opposed to gambling, the practice did not become common until some time after the introduction of the cards themselves. Possibly the Romany, or 'gypsies', came across the game of Tarocchi on their travels in Europe and decided to use the cards for fortune-telling. Or individuals developed the concept (the earliest written references are individual interpretations, though they might have derived from some earlier system, not written down but in general use) and the Romany took it from them. People used to believe that the Romany themselves brought the cards from Egypt. The fact is, the Romany probably came from India, and they arrived in Spain a good hundred years after Tarot cards were introduced in Italy and France.

In the section on readings we will consider just what divination does, and how such an outrageous practice could possibly work. Here we can simply observe that people can and have told fortunes with anything – the smoky innards of slaughtered beasts, bird patterns across the sky, coloured stones, tossed coins, anything. The practice stems from the simple desire to know, in advance, what is going to happen, and more subtly, from the inner conviction that everything is connected, everything has meaning and that nothing occurs at random.

The very idea of randomness is really very modern. It developed out of the dogma that cause and effect is the only valid connection between two events. Events without this logical joining are random, that is, meaningless. Previously, however, people thought in terms of 'correspondences'. Events or patterns in one area of existence corresponded to patterns in other areas. The pattern of the zodiac corresponds to the pattern of a person's life. The pattern of tea leaves in the bottom of a cup corresponds to the outcome of a battle. Everything is connected. The idea has always claimed its adherents, and recently even some scientists, impressed by the way events will occur in series (like a 'run of bad luck'), have begun to look seriously at it.

If we can use anything for fortune-telling why use the Tarot? The answer is, that any system will tell us *something*; the value of that something depends on the inherent wisdom of the system. Because the Tarot pictures carry deep significance all by themselves, the patterns they form in readings can teach us a great deal about ourselves, and life in general. Unfortunately, most diviners over the years have ignored these deeper meanings, preferring simple formulas ('a dark man, one disposed to help the querent'), easily interpreted and quickly digested by the client.

The formula meanings are often contradictory as well as blunt, with no indications of how to choose between them. This situation holds true especially for the Minor Arcana which is the bulk of the deck. Almost no works on the Tarot have treated this subject fully. Most serious studies, those which deal with the deep meanings of the Major Arcana, either do not mention the Minor cards at all, or simply throw in another set of formulas at the back, as a grudging addition for those readers who will insist on using the deck for fortune-telling. Even Waite, as mentioned, simply gives his own formulas to the remarkable pictures drawn by Pamela Smith.

While this book will deal extensively with the concepts embodied in the cards and their symbolism it will also look carefully at the application of these concepts to Tarot readings. Many writers, notably Waite, have denigrated divination as a degenerate use of the cards. But the proper use of readings can greatly increase our awareness of the cards' meanings. It is one thing to study the symbolism of a particular card, it is something else to see that card in combination with others. Many times I have seen specific readings open up important meanings that would not have emerged in any other way.

Readings teach us a general lesson as well, and a very important one. In a manner no explanation can possibly equal, they demonstrate that no card, no approach to life, is good or bad except in the context of the moment.

Finally, giving readings gives each person a chance to renew his or her instinctive feeling for the pictures themselves. All the symbolism, all the archetypes, all the explanations given in this book or any other can only prepare you to look at the pictures and say, 'This card tells me ...'.

Chapter 1.

The Four Card Pattern

Unity and Duality

hrough its long history the Major Arcana has attracted a great many interpretations. Today, we tend to look upon the trumps as a psychological process, one that shows us passing through different stages of existence to reach a state of full development; we can describe this state, for the moment, as unity with the world around us, or perhaps liberation from weakness, confusion, and fear. The full Arcana describes this process in detail, but to get an understanding of it as a whole we need look at only four cards; four basic archetypes arranged in a graphic pattern of evolution and spiritual awareness.

If you have your own deck of Rider Pack Tarot cards* remove the Fool, the Magician, the High Priestess, and the World, and place them in the diamond pattern shown overleaf. Look at them for a while. Notice that while both the Fool and the World show dancing, joyful figures, the Magician and the High Priestess are stationary and unmoving in their positions. If you glance through the rest of the Major Arcana you will notice that all the trumps but 0 and 21 are drawn as if staged for a still photograph, rather than say, a motion picture. They present themselves as fixed states of existence.

But there is a difference between the two dancers. The Fool rushes forward richly clothed; the figure in the World is naked. The Fool looks about to leap into the lower world from some high distant country; the World paradoxically appears outside the material universe, the Dancer suspended in a magical wreath of victory.

Note also the numbers of the four cards. 0 is not strictly a number

---

* In other decks, particularly those older than Waite's the Fool appears very different from the one shown here. The chapter on the symbolism of the Fool (page 24) will deal with this alternative tradition.

at all, rather it represents the absence of any specific number, and therefore we can say that it contains all numbers within itself. It symbolizes infinite potentiality. All things remain possible because no definite form has been taken. 1 and 2 are the first genuine numbers, the first reality; again, a fixed state. They form the archetypes 'odd' and 'even', and therefore represent all opposites, male and female, light and dark, passive and active, etc. But 21 combines these two numbers in one figure.

Look at their postures. The Magician raises a magic wand to heaven. Besides the ideas of spirit and unity, the phallic wand symbolizes maleness. The High Priestess sits between two pillars, a vaginal symbol as well as a symbol of duality. These two pillars appear again and again in the Major Arcana, in such obvious places as the temple in the Hierophant, and in more subtle ways, like the two lovers on card 6, or the two sphinxes harnessed to the Chariot. But now look at the World. The dancer, a female figure (though some decks represent her as a hermaphrodite) carries two magic wands, one in each hand. The male and female are unified, and more, their separate qualities are subordinated to the higher freedom and joy shone in the light way the dancer holds these powerful symbols.

Clearly, then, while the horizontal line, the Magician and the High Priestess, shows a duality of opposites, the vertical line, 0 and 21, shows a unity, the Fool being some sort of perfect state before duality, and the World giving us a glimpse of the exhilarating sense of freedom possible if only we can reconcile the opposites buried in our psyches.

The Tarot, like many systems of thought, indeed like many mythologies, symbolizes duality as the separation of male and female. The Qabalists believed that Adam was originally hermaphroditic, and that Eve only became separate from him as a result of the Fall. In most cultures, to a greater or lesser degree, men and women see each other as very distinct, almost separate societies. Today, many people think of each person as having both masculine and feminine qualities, but previously such an idea was found only in esoteric doctrines of unification.

If we picture duality dramatically as male and female, or black and white, we also experience more subtle splits in our ordinary lives, especially between our hopes, what we imagine as possible, and the reality of what we achieve. Very often the actions we take turn out not to fulfil our hopes for them. The marriage gives less than the total happiness expected, the job or career brings more frustration than fulfilment. Many artists have said that the paintings on the canvases are never the paintings they envisioned; they never can express what they really wanted to say. Somehow the reality of life is always less than the potential. Acutely aware of this, many people agonize over every decision, no matter how small or great, because they cannot accept that once they take an action in one direction they have lost the chance to go in all the other directions previously open to them. They cannot accept the limitations of acting in the real world.

The split between potentiality and reality is sometimes seen as the separation between mind and body. We sense that our thoughts and emotions are something distinct from our physical presence in the world. The mind is unlimited, able to go anywhere in the universe, backwards or forwards in time. The body is weak, subject to hunger, tiredness, sickness. Attempting to resolve this separation people have gone to philosophical extremes. Behaviourists have claimed that 'mind' does not exist; only the body and the habits it develops are real. At the other end, many mystics have experienced the body as an illusion created by our limited understanding. Christian tradition defines the 'soul' as the immortal 'true' self, existing before and after the body that contains it. And many religions and sects, such as the Gnostics and some Qabalists, have considered the body a prison, created by the sins or mistakes of our fallen ancestors.

At the source of all these dualities we feel we do not know ourselves. We sense that deep down our true nature is something stronger, freer, with great wisdom and power; or else a thing of violent passions and furious animal desire. Either way, we *know* that this true self hides, or perhaps lies buried deep inside our normal, socially restricted personalities. But how do we reach it? Assuming the essential self to be a thing of beauty and power, how do we liberate it?

The disciplines we call the 'occult sciences' begin with a strong awareness of all these splits and limitations. They then go on, however, to another idea, that there exists a key, or a plan, to bring everything together, to unify our lives with our hopes as we release our latent strength and wisdom. People often confuse the purposes of spiritual disciplines. Many think the Tarot is for fortune-telling, that alchemists want to become rich by changing lead to gold, that Qabalists work spells by saying secret words, and so on. In reality, these disciplines aim at a psychological unification. The 'base metal' that the alchemist wishes to change to gold is himself. Accepting the doctrine that we have fallen from a perfect state to a limited one the occultist does not believe we must simply wait passively for some future redemption by an outside agent. On the contrary, he or she believes it our responsibility to bring about that redemption by finding the key to unity.

The Tarot depicts a version of that 'key'. It is not *the* key, just as it is not really a secret doctrine. It represents a process, and one of the things it teaches us is that we make a mistake when we assume that unification comes through any simple key or formula. Rather, it comes through growth and increased awareness as we travel step by step through the twenty-one stages of the Major Arcana.

The Fool represents true innocence, a kind of perfect state of joy and freedom, a feeling of being one with the spirit of life at all times; in other words, the 'immortal' self we feel became entrapped in the confusions and compromises of the ordinary world. Perhaps such a radiant self never really existed. Somehow we experience our intuition of it as something lost. Virtually every culture has developed a myth of a Fall from a primeval paradise.

'Innocence' is a word often misunderstood. It does not mean 'without guilt' but rather a freedom and a total openness to life, a complete lack of fear that comes through a total faith in living and in your own instinctive self. Innocence does not mean 'asexual' as some people think. It is sexuality expressed without fear, without guilt, without connivance and dishonesty. It is sexuality expressed spontaneously and freely, as the expression of love and the ecstasy of life.

The Fool bears the number 0 because all things are possible to the person who is always ready to go in any direction. He does not belong in any specific place; he is not fixed like the other cards. His innocence makes him a person with no past, and therefore an infinite future. Every moment is a new starting point. In Arabic numerals the number 0 bears the shape of an egg, to indicate that all things emerge from it. Originally the zero was written as a dot; in Hermetic and Qabalistic tradition the universe emerged from a single point of light. And God in the Qabalah is often described as 'nothingness' because to describe God as any *thing* would be to limit Him to some finite fixed state. Those Tarot commentators who argue whether the Fool belongs before, after, or somewhere between the other cards seem to be missing the point. The Fool is movement, change, the constant leap through life.

For the Fool no difference exists between possibility and reality. 0 means a total emptiness of hopes and fears, and the Fool expects nothing, plans nothing. He responds instantly to the immediate situation.

Other people will receive his complete spontaneity. Nothing calculated, nothing held back. He does not do this deliberately, like someone consciously deciding to be wholly honest with a friend or a lover. The Fool gives his honesty and love naturally, to everyone, without ever thinking about it.

We speak of the Fool as 'he' and the World Dancer as 'she' because of their appearance in the pictures, but both can be a woman or a man with really no change. Just as the Fool does not experience a separateness from the physical world so he or she does not experience any isolation from the 'opposite sex'. The Fool and the Dancer are psychic hermaphrodites, expressing their complete humanity at all times, by their very natures.

Now look again at the four card pattern. See how the Fool splits into the Magician and the High Priestess, who must be brought back together again to form the World. The two cards represent the splitting up of the Fool's innocence into the illusion of opposites. The World shows us a restored unity, but a higher and deeper unity achieved through the growth outlined in the other eighteen cards. The fool is innocence, but the World is wisdom.

Innocence and Freedom

The Fool teaches us that life is simply a continuous dance of experience. But most of us cannot maintain even brief moments of such spontaneity and freedom. Due to fears, conditioning, and simply the very real problems of daily life, we necessarily allow our egos to isolate us from experience. Yet within us we can sense, dimly, the possibility of freedom, and therefore we call this vague feeling of a loss, a 'fall' from innocence. Once we lose that innocence, however, we cannot simply climb back to the level of the Fool. Instead, we must struggle and learn, through maturity, self-discovery, and spiritual awareness, until we reach the greater freedom of the World.

The Magician represents action, the High Priestess passivity, the Magician maleness, the High Priestess femaleness, the Magician consciousness, the High Priestess unconsciousness.

By 'consciousness' we do not mean the high awareness of the World, but rather the powerful yet limited consciousness of ego as it creates an outer universe of boundaries and forms. This description does not mean to denigrate or belittle the Magician's creative force. What greater creativity is there than giving shape to the chaos of experience? It is the Magician who gives life its meaning and purpose. Healers, artists, and occultists have all focused on the Magician as their patron card. Nevertheless, his power represents an isolation from the freedom of the Fool or the understanding of the World.

In the same way, the High Priestess indicates, in her unconsciousness, a very deep state of intuitive awareness. And yet, her inner knowledge does not belong to that radiant centre of nothingness that enables the Fool to act so freely.

The High Priestess represents the archetype of inner truth, but because this truth is unconscious, inexpressible, she can maintain it only through total passivity. This situation shows itself in life in numerous ways. We all carry within us a dim sense of who we are, of a genuine self never seen by other people and impossible to explain. But the women and men who throw themselves into competition, careers, responsibilities, without working at the same time to increase self-knowledge, often discover at some point that they have lost the sense of who they are, and what they once wanted in life. Now, directly opposite to these people, the Buddhist monk or nun withdraws from the world because the slightest involvement will distract them from the centre of their meditations.

Both the Magician and the High Priestess bear an archetypal purity. In a way, they have not lost the Fool's radiance, they have simply split it up into light and darkness. In the traditional split of

Western and Eastern religion the Magician represents the West, with its emphasis on action and historical salvation, the High Priestess the East, the way of separation from the world and time. Yet those who have gone deepest in both traditions will combine these elements.

The High Priestess sits between the pillars of light and dark. Though she herself symbolizes the dark passive side, her intuition can find a balance between the two. This is less paradoxical than it sounds. If we sense our lives as filled with opposites which we cannot resolve, we can react in either of two ways. We can rush back and forth, going from one extreme to the other, or we can do absolutely nothing. Sit in the middle, not seduced in either direction, but passive, allowing the opposites to go on around you. Except, of course, that this too is a choice, and eventually we lose that balance and that inner knowledge simply because life continues on around us.

In Qabalist imagery the High Priestess represents the Pillar of Harmony, a force which reconciles the opposing Pillars of Mercy and Judgement. Therefore she sits between the two pillars of the temple. But without the ability to blend in the active force of the Magician, the High Priestess's sense of harmony becomes swept away.

As archetypes, the Magician and the High Priestess cannot exist in our lives any more than the Fool can. Inevitably, we mix up these elements (rather than blend them) and thereby experience their lesser forms, as confused action, or else insecure and guilt ridden passivity. In other words, the purity of the two poles becomes lost because life muddles them together.

The purpose of the Major Arcana is twofold. First of all, by isolating the elements of our lives into archetypes it enables us to see them in their pure forms, as aspects of psychological truth. Secondly, it helps us to truly resolve these different elements, to take us step by step through the different stages of life until it brings us to unity. In reality, perhaps the innocence symbolized by the Fool never existed. Somehow we experience as something lost. The Major Arcana tells us how to get it back.

Chapter 2.
The Overview

The Cards as a Sequence

ost interpreters of the Major Arcana take one of two approaches: either they consider the cards as separate entities or they look at them as a sequence. The first approach looks at each card as representing different qualities or situations of importance to a person's spiritual development. The Empress represents the soul glorified in nature, the Emperor mastery of self, etc. This system considers the numbers on the cards as part of their symbolic language. The number 1 belongs to the Magician not because he comes first but because that number signifies ideas – unity, will power – appropriate to the concept of the Magician.

The second approach looks upon the trumps as a progression. The Magician is 1 because his qualities form the starting point of the growth pattern figured in the other cards. Card number 13, say, belongs at just that point, between the Hanged Man and Temperance, and no other. Each new trump builds upon the previous one and leads the way to the next.

In general, I have followed the second method. While the number symbolism should not be neglected it is equally important to see where each card fits in the overall pattern. Comparisons with other numbers can also help us to see the limitations as well as the virtues of each card. For instance, number 7, the Chariot, is often spoken of as 'victory'. But what kind of victory? Is it the total liberation of the World, or something narrower, but still of great value? Looking at the card's position can answer these questions.

The interpreters who have taken this approach have usually looked for some place to divide the trumps for easier comprehension. The most common choice is the Wheel of Fortune. As the number ten, it symbolizes a completion of one cycle and a beginning of another. Also, if you place the Fool at the beginning this divides the cards neatly into two groups of eleven. Most important, the idea of a turning wheel symbolizes a change of outlook, from a concern with external things, such as success and romance, to the more inward approach depicted in such cards as Death and the Star.

Despite the value of seeing the Major Arcana as two halves, I have found that the trumps divide even more organically into three parts. Setting the Fool apart as really a separate category all by itself (and setting it apart allows us to see that it belongs everywhere and anywhere) gives us twenty-one cards – three groups of seven.

The number seven has a long history in symbolism: the seven planets of classical astrology, seven as a combination of three and four, themselves archetypal numbers, seven pillars of wisdom, the seven lower stations of the Tree of Life, seven openings in the human head, seven chakras, and of course, seven days in the week.

One particular aspect of seven relates it directly to the Tarot. The Greek letter *pi* stands for a ratio that exists in all circles between the circumference and the diameter. No matter how large or small the circle, the two will always work out to the same fraction, 22/7. And the Major Arcana with the Fool comes to twenty-two, just as without the Fool it reduces to seven. Also, twenty-two times seven equals one hundred and fifty-four (154 adds up to ten, linking it to the Wheel), and one hundred and fifty-four divided by two, for the two Arcana, comes to seventy-seven, the entire Tarot with the Fool again set aside.

Like the Qabalistic conception of God the point is nothing, yet the entire circle radiates from it. And the Fool's number, 0, has been represented as a circle as well as a point.

The best reasons for the division into three groups lie within the Major Arcana itself. First, consider the picture symbolism. Look at the first card in each line. The Magician and Strength are both obviously cards of power, but so is the Devil. The Magician and Strength are linked by the infinity sign above their heads, while the Devil bears a reversed pentacle. If you look at the Devil's posture, one arm up, one arm down, you will see the picture is in some ways a parody of the Magician, with the torch pointing down instead of the wand pointing up. In some decks card 15 carries the title of 'Black Magician'. (In many decks Justice, not Strength is number 8. If you look at the posture of the figure in Justice you will see an even closer resemblance to the Magician and the Devil.) The same kind of vertical correspondences apply all the way through the three lines.

The Three Areas of Experience
The division into three allows us to see the Major Arcana as dealing with three distinct areas of experience. Briefly, we can call these:

consciousness, the outer concerns of life in society; subconscious, or the search inward to find out who we really are; and super-conscious, the development of a spiritual awareness and a release of archetypal energy. The three levels are not forced categories. They derive from the cards themselves.

The first line, with its concentration on such matters as love, social authority, and education, describes the main concerns of society. In many ways the world we see mirrored in our novels, films, and schools is summed up by the first seven cards of the Major Arcana. A person can live and die and be judged a success by everyone around him or her without ever going beyond the level of the Chariot. Many people, in fact, do not reach that level at all.

Modern depth psychology concerns itself with the second line of trumps, with their symbols of a hermit-like withdrawal into self-awareness followed by a symbolic Death and rebirth. The angel of Temperance at the end represents that part of ourselves which we discover to be essentially real after the illusions of ego, defensiveness, and rigid habits of the past are allowed to die away.

Finally, what of the last line? What can go beyond finding our true selves? To put it simply, these seven cards depict a confrontation and finally a unity with the great forces of life itself. The other cards, formerly seen as so important, become merely the preparation for the great descent into darkness, the liberation of light, and the return of that light to the sunlit world of consciousness.

To most readers the last line will seem too vague and fanciful. We can call this subject matter 'religious' or 'mythical' but these words too remain hard to grasp.

The vagueness in our minds perhaps speaks more about ourselves and our time than about the subject. Any society automatically teaches its people, just by the language it uses, to make certain assumptions about the world. Examples in our culture would include the value and uniqueness of individuals, the reality and overwhelming importance of love, the necessity of freedom and social justice, and, more complex, but just as strong, the basic separateness of each person. 'We are born alone and we die alone.' Our society, built upon the materialist eighteenth and nineteenth centuries, does not merely reject the notion of 'superconsciousness' or 'universal forces', we do not really know what they mean.

When we deal with the last line of the Major Arcana, then, we deal with an area uncomfortable to many of us. It will make the task of understanding these cards harder – and perhaps more rewarding. Working with these ancient pictures can bring us knowledge neglected in our education.

Chapter 3.

The Opening Trumps: Symbols and Archetypes

(a)   Figure 1   *(b)*

The Fool

We have already looked at the Fool in one aspect, the image of a spirit totally free. But we can look at the Fool from another side – the leap into the archetypal world of the trumps.

Imagine yourself entering a strange landscape. A world of magicians, of people hanging upside down, and of dancers in the bright air. You can enter through a leap from a height, through a dark cave, a labyrinth, or even by climbing down a rabbit hole chasing a Victorian rabbit with a pocket watch. Whichever way you choose, you are a fool to do it. Why look into the deep world of the mind when you can stay safely in the ordinary landscape of job, home and family? Herman Melville, in *Moby Dick*, warned his readers not to take even a step outside the ordinary path laid out for you by society. You might not get back again.

And yet, for those willing to take the chance, the leap can bring joy, adventure, and finally, for those with the courage to keep going when the wonderland becomes more fearsome than joyous, the leap can bring knowledge, peace, and liberation. Interestingly, the Fool archetype appears more in mythology than in structured religion. An institutionalized Church can hardly urge people beyond the limits of institutions. Instead, the churches offer us a safe haven from the fears of life. Mythology leads directly into the heart of those fears, and in every culture the mythological landscape contains the image of the Trickster – pushing, goading, jabbing the kings and heroes whenever they turn away from the inner world of truth.

In the King Arthur legends Merlin appears not only as a sorcerer and wise man but as a trickster. Constantly he appears before Arthur in disguise, as a child, a beggar, an old peasant. The young king, already seduced into pompousness by his high social position, never recognizes Merlin until his companions point out that he has been tricked again. More important than laws or military strategy is the ability to see through illusions. The Taoist masters were famous for playing tricks on their disciples.

The Fool archetype has even found social expression, as the real court jester. We all know the image from *King Lear* of 'the fool', permitted to tell the king truths no one else would dare to express. Today, our comedians and satirists enjoy something of the same privilege.

In many countries a yearly carnival releases all the wildness repressed through the rest of the year. Sex is freer, various laws are suspended, people go in disguises and the King of Fools is chosen to preside over the festival. Today, in Europe and North America, April the first remains 'April Fool's Day', a time for tricks and practical jokes.

The picture beside that of the Rider pack shows the Fool as conceived by Oswald Wirth. An older tradition than that of Waite, it pictures the archetype as a grotesque wanderer. This image has been interpreted variously as the soul before enlightenment, a newborn child entering the world of experience and the principle of anarchy. Elizabeth Haich has provided an interesting interpretation of Wirth's grotesque image of the Fool. Placing him between

Judgement and the World, she describes the Fool as what the outside world sees when it looks upon someone who is truly enlightened. Because the Fool does not follow their rules or share their weaknesses, he appears to them in this ugly distorted way. Haich describes the Fool's face as a mask, put there not by himself but by the outside world. The last card, the World, presents the same enlightened person, but viewed from inside, that is, by himself.

In some early Tarot decks the Fool appeared as a giant court jester, towering over the people around him. His title was 'the Fool of God'. The term has also been used for idiots, harmless madmen, and severe epileptics, all of whom were thought to be in touch with a greater wisdom precisely because they were out of touch with the rest of us.

The archetype persists in modern popular mythology as well. By their fantastic primitive nature comic books often reflect mythological themes better than novels. In *Batman* the hero's strongest enemy is called the Joker, a figure who has no past and is never seen without the wild make-up of a joker in a deck of cards. The joker, of course, descends directly from the Fool of tarochhi. The rivalry of Batman and the Joker sends a clear message to their readers: do not rebel against social values. Support law and order. In recent years the magazine has described the Joker as insane rather than criminal. To society the way of the Fool, instinct rather than rules, is a dangerous insanity.

So far we have looked at the Fool as the 'other', prodding us from complacency with his jokes and disguises. As the 'self' he represents that long tradition of the foolish brother or sister, despised by the older brothers and sisters, yet finally able to win the princess or the prince through instinctive wit and kindness.

Curiously the image of the Fool as self occurs more in fairy tales than myths. We look at myths as representing forces larger than ourselves; the simpler fairy tale allows us to express our own foolishness.

Like 'Boots' or 'Gluck' in the fairy tale, always accompanied by various animal helpers, the Fool in almost every deck walks with a companion. In Waite the figure is a leaping dog, in others a cat or even a crocodile. The animal symbolizes the forces of nature and the animal self of man, all in harmony with the spirit who acts from instinct. Mythological dogs are often terrifying, for example, the Hound of Hell chasing lost souls. But it is really the same beast; only our attitude changes. Deny your inner self and it becomes ferocious. Obey it and it becomes benign.

Waite's Fool holds a white rose. Roses symbolize passion, while white, the traditional colour of purity, together with the delicate way the flower is held, indicate the passions raised to a higher level. The Greeks saw Eros, the god of love, as a trickster, making the most proper people act ridiculous. But those who already express their folly will not be thrown by love. The Greeks also spoke of Eros, in other forms, as the animating force of the universe.

The bag behind him carries his experiences. He does not abandon them, he is not mindless, they simply do not control him in the way that our memories and traumas so often control our lives. The bag bears the head of an eagle, symbol of the soaring spirit. His high instinct fills and transforms all experience. The eagle is also the symbol of Scorpio raised to a higher level, that is, sexuality raised to spirit. This idea of the connection between sex and spirit will come up again with the card of the Devil.

Over his shoulder the Fool carries a stick, like a tramp. But this stick is actually a wand, symbol of power. The Magician and the Chariot driver also carry wands, but self-consciously, with a powerful grip. The Fool and the World Dancer hold their wands so casually we hardly notice them. What could be more foolish than to take a magic wand and use it to carry your bags? We can imagine a fairy tale in which the foolish younger brother finds a stick by the side of the road and carries it, not recognizing it as the lost wand of a wizard, and therefore not being destroyed like his two older brothers who tried to wield it for their own profit.

The Fool's wand is black; the others are white. For the unconscious Fool the spirit force remains always in potential, always ready, because he is not consciously directing it. We tend to misunderstand the colour black, seeing it as evil, or negation of life. Rather, black means all things being possible, infinite energy of life before consciousness has constructed any boundaries. When we fear blackness or darkness we fear the deep unconscious source of life itself.

Like the joker, the Fool really belongs anywhere in the deck, in combination with and between any of the other cards. He is the animating force giving life to the static images. In the Major Arcana he belongs wherever there is a difficult transition. Hence his position at the beginning, where there is the transition from the everyday world of the Minor Arcana to the world of archetypes. The Fool also helps us jump the gap from one line to the next, that is, from the Chariot to Strength, from Temperance to the Devil. To reach the Chariot or Temperance requires great effort and courage, and without the Fool's readiness to leap into new territory we would likely stop with what we have already achieved.

The Fool belongs as well with those cards of difficult passage, such as the Moon and Death (observe the winding road on each of these two), where he urges us on despite our fears.

In the Minor Arcana the Fool relates first of all to Wands – action, eagerness, movement without thought. But it connects as well to Cups, with their emphasis on imagination and instinct. The Fool, in fact, combines these two suits. Later we will see that this combination, fire and water, represents the way of transformation.

Finally the question arises of the Fool's place in divinatory readings. I have already mentioned the importance of readings for a fuller understanding of the cards. Even more, they help us apply the wisdom of the cards to our daily lives. In readings the Fool speaks to us of courage and optimism, urging faith in ourselves and in life. At difficult times, when we come under pressure from people around us to be practical, the Fool reminds us that our own inner selves can best tell us what to do.

The Fool can often symbolize beginnings, courageously leaping off into some new phase of life, particularly when that leap is taken from some deep feeling rather than careful planning.

These belong to the Fool in its normal position. We must also consider the 'reversed' meanings, that is, when the way we have mixed the cards makes the Fool come out with the feet on the top. Reversed meanings are controversial among Tarot commentators. Those who give formulas as meanings usually just turn the formula around, a simplistic method which has led several interpreters to abandon the whole idea of reversed meanings. But we can also look at reversals as deepening the meaning of the card as a whole. In general, a reversed card indicates that the qualities of that card have become blocked, distorted or channelled in another direction.

For the Fool a reversal means first of all a failure to follow your instincts. It can mean not taking a chance at some crucial time, because of fear or depending too much on plans and the practical advice of others.

Another reversed meaning of the Fool will appear at first to contradict the one just given. Recklessness, wildness, crazy schemes all seem the opposite of over-caution. And yet, they originate from the same weakness, a failure to act from inside. The reckless person superimposes a conscious or artificial foolishness on his life both because he does not trust the unconscious to act as a guide and because is also afraid of doing nothing.

This second reversed meaning suggests another dimension to the Fool – the awareness that great chances must be taken only at the proper time. There are, after all, many times when caution is needed, and times when it is better to do nothing at all. The basic thing any oracle teaches us is that no action or attitude is right or wrong, except in its proper context.

As we go further into the Tarot we will see that this concept of the proper time permeates the cards and is, in fact, the true key to their correct use. The card in the Rider pack that falls exactly in the middle of the three lines, that is, Justice, means a proper response.

Figure 2

The Magician

The Magician emerges very directly from the Fool in the image of the trickster-wizard. As mentioned above, Merlin fulfils both these roles (as well as that of teacher and wise man), and many other myths make the same connection. Earlier Tarot decks pictured trump number one as a conjurer rather than a magus, or even a juggler tossing coloured balls in the air. Charles Williams described him as a juggler tossing the stars and planets.

Most modern images of the trump follow Waite's wizard, raising a magic wand to bring into reality the spirit force – the energy of life in its most creative form. He holds the wand carefully, aware of that psychic power the Fool carried so lightly on his shoulder. Thus, the Magician, as the beginning of the Major Arcana proper, represents consciousness, action and creation. He symbolizes the idea of manifestation, that is, making something real out of the possibilities in life. Therefore, we see the four emblems of the Minor Arcana – lying on a table in front of him. He not only uses the physical world for his magical operations (the four emblems are all objects used by wizards in their rituals), but he also creates the world, in the sense of giving life a meaning and direction.

The Magician stands surrounded by flowers to remind us that the emotional and creative power we feel in our lives needs to be grounded in physical reality for us to get any value from it. Unless we make something of our potentials they do not really exist.

'In the beginning, God created the heaven and the earth.' The Bible begins at the moment the spirit descends into physical reality. For us, in the physical world, we can talk of nothing before this moment. In the linking of the Tarot with the Hebrew alphabet the Fool often receives the first letter *Aleph*. (*Aleph* bears no sound; it is a silent carrier of vowels, and therefore symbolizes nothingness. It is the first letter of the Ten Commandments.) This would assign the second Hebrew letter, *Beth*, the first letter with an actual sound, to the Magician. *Beth* is the first letter of Genesis.

Look at Waite's picture of the Magician. He is not casting spells, or conjuring up demons. He simply stands with one hand raised to heaven and the other pointed to the green earth. He is a lightning rod. By opening himself up to the spirit he draws it down into himself, and then that downward hand, like a lightning rod buried in the ground, runs the energy into the earth. Into reality.

We see many accounts of the 'descent of the spirit' in the Bible, in other religious texts and in contemporary religious experience. People 'speak in tongues' in Pentecostal churches, they scream and shout and roll on the floor at Gospel meetings. The priest giving communion sees himself as a 'vessel' or channel for the Holy Ghost. But we can see this experience in much simpler, non-religious, terms as well. People tremble with excitement at sporting events. 'I'm so excited I could burst!' In a new love affair or at the start of a new career, we feel a power filling us. You can sometimes see people at the opening of some important phase of their lives, tapping their legs up and down, half bouncing in their seats, filled with some energy they cannot seem to discharge. And writers and artists, when their work is going well, will experience themselves as almost passive channels for a spirit-like force. The word 'inspiration' originally meant 'filled with a holy breath', and derives from the same root as 'spirit'.

Notice that of all these examples all but the priest and the artist are seized with a frenzy. The possessed church-goer and the teenager about to burst at a football game share the feeling that their bodies are overwhelmed by a power too great for it. Far from being gentle the surge of energy can be almost painful. The person in religious fervour shouts and leaps about in order to release an unbearable energy.

The life force that fills the universe is not gentle or benign. It must be discharged, grounded in something real, because our bodies, our selves, are not meant to contain it, but only pass it on. Thus, the artist does not join in the physical frenzy because she or he is discharging that power into the painting. Similarly the priest passes the power into the bread and wine.

We function best as a channel for energy. Unless we follow the path of the High Priestess in withdrawing from the world, we live our lives most fully when we create or are active. 'Create' does not mean simply art, but any activity that produces something real and valuable outside of ourselves.

Many people experience feelings of being powerful so infrequently they try to hold on to them. By doing nothing they hope to preserve their magic moments. But we can really hold on to power in our lives only by constantly discharging it. By releasing creative power we open ourselves up to receive a further flow. However, by trying to hold on to it, we block the channels and the sense of power, which is really life itself, withers within us. The spectator at the football game, even the possessed church-goer, will find their excitement gone after the event that triggered it has ended. But the craftsman or scientist or teacher – or, for that matter, the Tarot reader – will find the power increase over the years the more they discharge it into physical reality.

When we look at the Magician those of us who feel a lack or a flatness in our lives will be drawn to the wand raised towards heaven. But the real magic rests in that finger pointing to the earth. That ability to create gives him his title. His image stems not only from the trickster-conjurer, but also from the archetypal hero. In our culture this would be Prometheus, who brought the heavenly fire down to weak and cold humanity.

In the West we tend to see wizards as manipulators. They learn secret techniques or make deals with Satan in order to gain personal power. This somewhat decadent image comes partly from the magicians themselves, since they make charms to find buried treasure, but also from the Church, which sees magicians, who deal directly with the spirit instead of going through the official priesthood, as competitors. The Tarot and all occult sciences are in a sense revoltionary, because they teach direct salvation, in this life, through your own efforts.

We can get a different concept of the Magician through the image of the shaman, or medicine man. Because no hierarchical Church has arisen to banish the shamans they have not become isolated from the community. They serve as healers, teachers, and directors of the soul after death. Like the wizards, the shamans study and learn complicated techniques. Their magical vocabulary is often much larger than the everyday vocabulary of the people around them. None of this training, however, is used to manipulate the spirit or for personal gain. Rather, the shaman only seeks to become a proper channel, both for himself so he will not be overwhelmed, and for the community so he can serve them better. He knows the great power that will enter him at moments of ecstasy and he wants to make sure it does not destroy him and make him of no use to the people around him.

Like the wizard the shaman has developed his will to the point where he can direct the fire that fills him. At the same time he remains open, allowing his ego to dissolve under the direct onslaught of the spirit. It says something about our culture that our wizards stand inside magic circles to make sure the demons cannot touch them.

We can apply the shaman attitude to our use of the whole Tarot deck. We study the cards, learn the symbolic language, even specific formulas, in order to give a direction to the feelings they arouse in us. But we must not forget that the true magic lies in the images themselves and not the explanations.

The divinatory meanings of the Magician derive from both hands, the one which receives the power and the one which directs. The card means first of all an awareness of power in your life, of spirit or simple excitement possessing you. It can also mean, depending on its position and your reaction to it, someone else's power affecting you. Like the Fool, the card refers to beginnings, but here the first actual steps. It can mean both the inspiration to begin some new project or phase of life, and the excitement that sustains you through the hard work to reach your goal. For many people the Magician can become a strong personal symbol for the creative force throughout their lives.

Secondly, the Magician means will-power; the will unified and directed towards goals. It means having great strength because all your energy is channelled in a specific direction. People who seem always to get what they want in life are often people who simply know what they want and can direct their energy. The Magician teaches us that both will-power and success derive from being conscious of the power available to everyone. Most people rarely act; instead they react, being knocked from one experience to the next. To act is to direct your strength, through the will, to the places where you want it to go.

The Magician reversed signifies that in some way the proper flow of energy has become disrupted or blocked. It can mean a weakness, a lack of will or a confusion of purpose that leads to doing nothing.

The power is there, but we cannot touch it. The card reversed can mean the lethargic apathy that characterizes depression.

The reversed trump can also mean power abused, a person who uses his or her very strong character to exert a destructive influence on others. The most direct example of this would of course be the psychic aggression of 'black magic'.

Finally, the Magician reversed indicates mental disquiet, hallucinations, fear and particularly fear of madness. This problem arises when the energy or spirit fire enters a person who does not know how to direct it into an outer reality. If we do not ground the lightning it can become trapped in the body and force itself on our awareness as anxiety or hallucinations. Anyone who has ever gone through a moment of total panic will know that acute mental anxiety is a very physical experience, a feeling of the body running wild, like a fire out of control. The word 'panic' means 'possessed by the god Pan', himself a symbol of magical forces.

Think again of the lightning rod. It not only attracts the bolt but runs it into the dirt. Without that connection to the earth the lightning would burn down the house.

Several writers have commented on the relationship between shamanism and what the West calls 'schizophrenia'. Shamans are often not so much chosen as found. If, in our culture, a young person experiences visions, fearful hallucinations, we do not know what to do with such experiences other than to try and stop them, by drugs and self-control. But in other cultures, such people receive training. This is not to say that madness does not exist or is not recognized in archaic cultures. Rather, the training is meant to prevent madness by channelling the experiences into a productive direction.

The initiates learn, through study with an established shaman, and through physical techniques such as fasting, how to understand, structure and finally direct these visionary experiences towards the service of the community. The Magician reversed should not be banished or confined; instead, we must find the way to turn it right side up.

Figure 3

The High Priestess

Bill Butler, in *The Definitive Tarot* has commented on the historical-legendary sources for this female archetype. Throughout the Middle Ages the story persisted that a woman was once elected Pope. Disguised for years as a man, this supposed 'Pope Joan' made her way through the Church hierarchy to the top position, only to die in childbirth during an Easter celebration.

Pope Joan was most likely a legend; the Visconti Papess was real. In the late thirteenth century an Italian group called the Guglielmites believed that their founder, Guglielma of Bohemia, who died in 1281, would rise again in 1300 and begin a new age in which women would be popes. Jumping ahead they elected a woman named Manfreda Visconti as the first papess. The Church graphically ended this heresy by burning Sister Manfreda in 1300, the year of the expected new age. Some hundred years later the same Visconti family commissioned the first set of Tarot cards as we know them. Among these unnumbered and unnamed trumps appeared a picture of a woman later decks titled 'The Papess'.

The name persisted until the eighteenth century when Court de Gebelin, believing the Tarot to originate in the Isis religion of ancient Egypt, changed the name to the High Priestess. Today both names exist (as well as 'Veiled Isis'), and the Waite image of the card derives directly from the Isis priestess's symbolic clothing, particularly the crown representing the three phases of the moon.

The Pope Joan legend and Manfreda Visconti are not simply historical curiosities. They illustrate a major social development in the Middle Ages, the reintroduction of the female and feminine principles into religion and cosmology. The images and the concepts associated with the masculine role had dominated both the Church and Jewish religion for centuries. As a result ordinary people experienced the religions of the priests and rabbis as remote, harsh, and unapproachable, with their emphasis on sin, judgement, and punishment. They wanted qualities of mercy and love. And they identified these with women. Like a mother shelters her child from the somewhat distant strictness of the father, a female diety supposedly would intrude for the pathetic sinners against the unremitting judgement of the Father.

It is interesting to realize that in many ways the Church saw Christ, as the Son, in exactly that role of introducing love and compassion. Yet, the people demanded a female. Even the idea of the Church as 'Mother Church' did not go far enough. Finally, the Church capitulated by raising the Virgin Mary almost to the level of Christ himself.

Many writers and scholars believe that the elevation of Mary – as well as the priests' costume of long skirts – originated in the Church's desire to assimilate a persistent goddess religion from the days before Christianity. If this is true it would indicate not so much a cultural conservatism as the power of the female archetype to maintain a hold and partially triumph against suppression.

In Judaism the official religion of the rabbis managed to resist any insurgent feminism. The people's need, however, took hold in another area: the long tradition of the Qabalah. The Qabalists took a term from the Talmud, 'Shekinah', which meant God's glory manifest in the physical world, and revised it to make it God's anima, or female side. The Qabalists also revised the idea of Adam, making him originally hermaphroditic. The separation of Eve from Adam, even the separation of the Shekinah from God, became results of the Fall; the absence of the female from the official religion became almost a matter of sin rather than purity.

So far we have looked at the benign motherly qualities of female mythological figures. Historically, however, female deities have always shown a dark, hidden side as well. To introduce the female at all is to introduce the whole archetype. The Tarot splits up the feminine archetype into two trumps and actually assigns the benign qualities to the second one (trump 3), the Empress. The High Priestess herself represents a deeper, more subtle aspect of the female; that of the dark, the mysterious and the hidden. As such, she connects to the virgin side of the Virgin Mary, the pure daughter side of the Shekinah (who was pictured simultaneously as mother, wife, and daughter).

We should realize that this assigning of qualities to women comes mostly from men and male ideas. The Qabalists, the occultists, and the Tarot designers, all deplored the separation of men and women into categories and taught unification as a final goal. This is shown by the World dancer of the Tarot. They were ahead of the established religion which even debated whether women had souls at all. Nevertheless, men still made the categories. To men, women have always appeared mysterious, strange, and, when safely in their mother role, loving and merciful. Women seem alien to men, more subtle in their thinking and non-rational. In our time, constant novels and films have pictured simple men manipulated by cunning women.

The fact that the menstrual cycle lasts about as long as the lunar cycle links women to that remote silvery body. Menstruation itself, a copious bleeding from the genitals, with no loss of life, has simply terrified men through the centuries. Even today superstitious Jews believe that one drop of menstrual blood will kill a plant. The fearful mystery of birth further connected women to the idea of darkness. The foetus grows and the soul enters it in the warm moist darkness of the womb. Motherhood linked women to the earth, and there too darkness dominates. Seeds lie in the ground through the dark dead winter, to emerge as food under the warm reassuring rays of the sun which, in many cultures, is considered as male.

Just as the sun's rays penetrate the earth so the male organ penetrates the female to leave a seed in her mysterious womb. We can easily see how men came to view themselves as active and women as both passive and mysterious. People often link passive with 'negative' or that is, inferior and weak. But passivity contains its own power. It gives the mind a chance to work. People who only know action never get a chance to reflect on what that action has taught them. In a deeper sense, passivity allows the subconscious to emerge. Only through withdrawal from outer involvement can we allow the inner voice of vision and psychic forces to speak to us. It is precisely to avoid this inner voice that many people never rest from action and movement. Our society, based completely on outer achievement, fosters a terror of the subconscious; yet without its wisdom we can never fully know ourselves or the world.

The High Priestess represents all these qualities: darkness, mystery, psychic forces, the power of the moon to stir the subconscious, passivity, and the wisdom gained from it. This wisdom cannot be expressed in rational terms; to try to do so would be to immediately limit, narrow, and falsify it. Most people at some time have felt they understood something in such a deep way that they could never manage to explain it. Myths serve as metaphors for deep psychic feelings; yet the myths themselves, like the explanations given by theologians and anthropologists, are only symbols. The High Priestess signifies inner wisdom at its deepest level.

She sits before two pillars, representing both the temple of Isis and the ancient Hebrew temple in Jerusalem, the dwelling place of God on earth, in other words, the home of the Shekinah. A veil hangs between the two pillars, indicating that we are barred from entering the place of wisdom. The image of the veiled temple or sanctuary appears in many religions. The Shekinah was indeed said to dwell within the veiled ark of the temple.

Now, most people assume we are somehow forbidden to pass the pillars of the High Priestess. In reality, we simply do not know how to. To enter behind the veil would be to know consciously the irrational wisdom of the unconscious. That is the goal of the entire Major Arcana. Look carefully at Smith's picture. You can see what lies behind the veil by looking between the veil and the pillars. And what lies behind is water. No great temple or complex symbols, simply a pool of water, a line of hills, and the sky. The pool signifies the unconscious and the truth hidden there. The water is motionless, the secrets in its darkest depths, hidden under a smooth surface. For most of us, at most times, the turbulent subconscious remains hidden under a placid layer of consciousness. We cannot enter the temple because we do not know how to go into ourselves; therefore we must travel through the trumps until we reach the Star and the Moon, where we can finally stir up the waters and return with the wisdom to the conscious light of the Sun.

The temple introduces the image of the two pillars, and the theme of duality and opposites. The image occurs again and again through the trumps, in such obvious places as the Hierophant's church pillars or the two towers of the Moon (the pillars of the High Priestess seen from the other side), but also in more subtle ways, such as the two sphinxes of the Chariot, or the man and woman of the Lovers. Finally, Judgement, with the child rising between a man and a woman, and the World, holding two wands, resolves the duality by uniting the inner mysteries with the outer awareness.

The letters 'B' and 'J' stand for Boaz and Jakin, the names given to the two main pillars of the temple in Jerusalem. Obviously, the dark Boaz stands for passivity and mystery while Jakin symbolizes action and consciousness. Notice, though, that the letters carry the reverse indications, a white B and a black J. Like the dots in the Tao symbol the letters signify that duality is an illusion, and each extreme carries the other imbedded inside it.

In her lap she holds a scroll marked 'Tora'. This name refers to the Jewish law, the Five Books of Moses which is usually spelled 'Torah' in English. This particular spelling allows the word to serve as an anagram for 'Taro'. As the ultimate subject of all Qabalistic meditations (like Christ's crucifixion for Christian mystics) the Torah carries a great deal of esoteric significance. The Qabalists believed that the Torah read on Saturday mornings in the synagogues was only a representation, a kind of shadow of the true Torah, the living word of God that existed before the universe and contains within it all true existence. The Tora held by the High Priestess, rolled up and partly concealed in her cloak, therefore signifies a higher knowledge closed to us with our lower understanding. We can describe it also as the psychic truths available to us only in the distorted form of myths and dreams.

Earlier we spoke of the Fool coming in at crucial moments of change to push us along. The gap between the High Priestess and the Empress is one such moment. We can too easily be seduced by the dark coolness of the second trump, even if we never really penetrate its secrets. The person beginning in spiritual discipline often prefers to stay at the visionary level rather than go through the slow hard work needed to advance. Many people in more ordinary situations will find life too overwhelming, too vast and demanding, for them to take part. We can best use the High Priestess's passivity as a balance to the outward-looking attitude of the Magician, but many people find the passive side extremely attractive. It represents an answer to struggle, a quiet retreat instead of the harsh glare of self-exposure when we involve ourselves openly with other people.

But the human mind does not work like that. It requires passion and it needs to connect itself to the world. If we cannot penetrate the veil the temple remains for us an empty place, devoid of meaning. The person who tries to live a completely passive life becomes depressed, more and more trapped in a cycle of apathy and fear.

Virtually all moon goddess religions feature myths of the goddess's ferocious side. Ovid tells the story of Actaeon, a hunter, and therefore a figure who properly belonged to the world of action. He happened one day to see a stream and decided to follow it to its source (again, water as a symbol of the unconscious). Thus he became separated from his dogs and the other hunters, and when he had reached the source, away from the active world, he saw a group of maidens. Among them, naked, stood the virgin goddess, Diana. Now, if Actaeon had returned immediately to the outer world he would have found his life enriched. Instead, he allowed Diana's beauty to fascinate him; he stayed too long, and the goddess, discovering that a man had seen her nakedness (compare the High Priestess's layers of clothing with the Star maiden's nudity) turned Actaeon into a stag. When he ran away, terrified, his own dogs tore him to pieces.

Here the Fool comes in (and remember the Fool's dog, leaping at his side), reminding us to dance lightly away from both these visions, the Magician as well as the High Priestess, until we are truly ready to assimilate them.

The divinatory meanings of the High Priestess deal first with a sense of mystery in life, both things we do not know, and things we cannot know. It indicates a sense of darkness, sometimes as an area of fear in our lives, but also one of beauty. A period of passive withdrawal can enrich our lives by allowing things inside to awaken.

As an emblem of secret knowledge the trump indicates that feeling of intuitively understanding the answer to some great problem, if only we could express that answer consciously. More specifically, the card can refer to visions and to occult and psychic powers, such as clairvoyance.

In its most positive aspect the High Priestess signifies the potential in our lives – very strong possibilities we have not realized, though we can sense them as possible. Action must follow or the potential will never be realized.

Despite its deep wisdom the card can sometimes carry a negative meaning. Like most of the trumps, the High Priestess's value depends on the context of the other cards. Negatively the trump indicates passiveness at the wrong time or for too long, leading to weakness, fear of life and other people. It shows a person with strong intuition who cannot translate feelings into action, or a person afraid to open up to other people. Whether the good or bad aspect of the card comes up in a particular reading depends on the surrounding cards and of course the reader's intuition (we partake of the High Priestess every time we read the cards). Very often both meanings will apply. Human beings have more than one side.

The High Priestess is an archetype, a single minded picture of one aspect of existence. When we reverse it we bring in the missing qualities. The card reversed signifies a turn towards passion, towards a deep involvement with life and other people, in all ways, emotionally, sexually and competitively. However, the pendulum can swing too far, and then the card reversed can symbolize a loss of that most precious knowledge: the sense of our inner selves.

Chapter 4.
The Worldly Sequence

The Major Arcana and Personal Growth

he first line of the Major Arcana takes us through the process of maturity. It shows the stages of a person's growth from a child, to whom mother is all loving and father all powerful, through, education, to the point where the child becomes an independent personality. At the same time these cards deal with a much wider development, of which the individual development is a microcosm. They depict the creation of human society, out of both the archetypes of existence and the chaotic energy of nature.

While they set the principles for the whole deck, the Magician and the High Priestess apply very specifically to the first line. The movement between opposites is the basic rhythm of the material world. Nothing exists absolutely in nature. In the words of Ursula Le Guin, 'Light is the left hand of darkness and darkness the right hand of light'. When we move from the two principles to the Empress we are seeing the opposites mingle together in nature to produce the reality of the physical universe.

The middle three cards of the line are a set. They show us a triad of nature, society, and the Church. They also signify mother, father, and education. In ancient Egypt the godhead was often viewed as a trinity. The persons changed from place to place and through the years, but they were usually a female and two males, with the female viewed as supreme. In the Tarot, nature, symbolized by the Empress, is the underlying reality, while her consorts, symbolized by the Emperor and the Hierophant, are human constructs.

The last two cards of the line represent the problems of the individual, love and sorrow, surrender and will. At some point each one of us must learn to distinguish ourselves from the outer world. Before this time personality remains a vague and formless creation of parents and society. Those who never make the break become cut off from a full life. For most people the medium by which they break from their parents is the emergence (Freudians and perhaps occultists would say 're-emergence') of the sexual drive at puberty. It is no accident that children rebel from their parents in ideas, habits, and dress at the same time that their bodies grow towards maturity.

The development of individuality is only a part of growth. Each person must find his or her personal goals and achievements. At the same time he or she will sooner or later face sorrow, sickness, and the general weakness of a life governed by old age and death. Only when we reach a full understanding of the outer life of humanity can we hope to reach inwards for a deeper reality.

Figure 4

The Empress

As stated in the previous chapter the Empress represents the more accessible, more benign aspects of the female archetype. She is motherhood, love, gentleness. At the same time she signifies sexuality, emotion and the female as mistress. Both motherhood and sex derive from feelings that are non-intellectual and basic to life. Passions rather than ideas. The High Priestess represented the mental side of the female archetype; her deep intuitive understanding. The Empress is pure emotion.

Like the Cunning Woman, we see her reflected in our movies and novels as the exasperating female, who both frustrates and delights, because her thought processes follow no rational development. Many women find this image insulting, partly because it represents values and approaches judged as negative by our patriarchal society, and partly because people make the error of assuming that women and men should personally express these archetypal ideas. But the social images are crippling in another way as well. They are trivial. The Empress, along with such mythological counterparts as Aphrodite or Ishtar or Erzulie, represent something very grand. They signify the passionate approach to life. They give and take experience with uncontrolled feeling.

Until we learn to experience the outer world completely we cannot hope to transcend it. Therefore the first step to enlightenment is sensuality. Only through passion, can we sense, from deep inside rather than through intellectual argument, the spirit that fills all existence.

Many people see religion as an alternative to the natural world, which they view as somehow impure or dirty. Though our cultural tradition fosters this duality it is really an illusion, and the person who approaches spirituality with this motivation to escape will likely never achieve a very developed understanding. The body, and the natural world, are realities that must be integrated rather than denied.

In the mythology of Buddhism we find that the gods manipulated Prince Siddhartha's father into providing his son, Gantama, with every sensual satisfaction. The father believed that pleasure would prevent his son from renouncing the world and becoming a Buddha. The scheme backfired, because only after he had completely experienced sensuality could the prince leave it behind. After renouncing the world Gautama joined the ascetics, the other pole. But he reached enlightenment only when he had rejected both extremes for the Middle Way. Thus, we can see the Buddha in the World dancer who holds both the Magician and the High Priestess lightly in her hands.

As a combination of 1 and 2 the number 3 signifies synthesis and harmony. The natural world combines the Magician and the High Priestess in an indivisible unity of life and death, darkness and light. The idea of emotion also brings together the Magician archetype of activeness with the High Priestess archetype of instinct.

Consider as well the process of creation. The Magician symbolizes the energy of life, the High Priestess the possibilities of future development. The reality of the Empress results from their combination. Recently Carl Sagan demonstrated that life on earth might have begun when a lightning bolt struck the primordial sea. Thus again, from the lightning of the Magician striking the waters of the High Priestess, comes the natural world.

The symbolism of the Waite-Smith Empress reflects the idea of nature, with all its force and glory. The Empress herself, voluptuous and sensual, suggests passion. Her shield is a heart with the sign of Venus, the Roman version of the Great Goddess. Throughout the ancient world the goddess ruled, as Demeter, Astarte, Nut, until the patriarchal invaders demoted her to wife (and finally banished her altogether with an all-male godhead). At the Empress's feet grows a field of grain; the goddess ruled agriculture, and in North-Western Europe was called the 'Corn Goddess'. She wears a necklace of nine pearls, for the nine planets, while her crown contains twelve stars for the signs of the zodiac. In short, she wears the universe as her jewellery. The Great Mother is not the forms of nature, but the underlying principle of life. The stars are six-pointed, a symbol much older than its current use as a social emblem for Judaism. The six-pointed star combines two triangles; the upwards one symbolizes fire, the downwards one water. Again, the Empress combines trumps 1 and 2 in a new reality.

A river flows from the trees behind her to disappear beneath her seat. This river is the force of life, running like a great current beneath all the separate forms of reality, and experienced most fully when we give ourselves to unrestrained passion. Deep in our selves we can sense the rhythm of a river, carrying us forward through experience until, with death, our individual lives return to the sea of existence.

The river symbolizes also the unity of change and stability. The water in it is never the same, yet it always remains a particular river, with its own special qualities. Human beings change from day to day, the cells of our bodies die and new ones take their place, yet we always remain ourselves.

The number 3 produced by the combination of 1 and 2 brings out yet another idea. Just as the numbers 1 and 2 stood specifically for male and female, so the number 3 signifies the child produced by their joining together. The child is born as a creature of nature, unburdened with ego and personality, experiencing the universe directly, without controls or labels. It is only as we grow older that we learn to put barriers between ourselves and life. It is one of the goals of the Tarot to return us to that natural state of directly experiencing the world around us.

But if the Empress signifies the child she also stands for the mother. Motherhood is the basic means by which life continues throughout nature. And because the physical bond of the mother and child is so direct, mother love, in its strongest form, is pure feeling, given without intellectual or moral considerations. (This is, of course, an ideal, and in reality such love may come more from the male parent than the female, or sadly, not at all.) Throughout history people have identified motherhood with nature, so that the term 'Great Mother' for the earth itself appears all over the world, and even today we speak vaguely of Mother Nature.

In readings the Empress represents a time of passion, a period when we approach life through feelings and pleasure rather than thought. The passion is sexual or motherly; either way it is deeply experienced, and in the right context can give great satisfaction. In the wrong context, when analysis is needed, the Empress can mean a stubborn emotional approach, a refusal to consider the facts. She can indicate another problem as well: self-indulgent pleasure when restraint is needed. Usually, however, she indicates satisfaction and even understanding gained through the emotions. The reversed meanings of the cards also have their positive and negative contexts. On the one hand it can signify a retreat from feeling, either rejecting your emotions or attempting to suppress your desires, particularly sexual. However, just as the High Priestess, upside down, added the missing element of involvement, so the Empress reversed can mean a new intellectual awareness, especially the solving of some complicated emotional problem by calmly thinking it through.

In their right side up and reversed meanings trumps 2 and 3 are mirrors of each other. It sometimes happens that in a reading both will appear, upside down. This means that the person expresses both emotional and intuitive mental aspects, but in a negative way. Rationality comes as a reaction to excessive emotional involvement, while a feeling of isolation or coldness leads to passion. If the two aspects of the goddess can be experienced right side up the person will achieve a more stable and rewarding balance.

(a)   Figure 5   (b)

The Emperor

For each child its parents are archetypes. Not just mother and father, but Mother and Father. Because our mothers give us life and feed us and shelter us we tend to see them as figures of love and mercy (and get very upset when they act harshly or coldly). But the Father, especially in traditional times when the sex roles were stricter, remained more remote, and therefore a figure of severity. It was the father who bore the authority and thus became the judge, the father who punished (and the mother who intervened) and the father who taught us the rules of society and then demanded obedience. To the child the father is in many ways indistinguishable from society as a whole, just as the mother is nature itself. One of the painful moments of maturity for many people comes when they discover the limited humanity of their parents.

In Freud's scheme of the mental development of the mate the father and the rules of society become directly linked. The infant psyche demands constant satisfaction, particularly in its desires for food and physical pleasure from the mother. (Freudians may claim the child desires actual intercourse with its mother, but the situation holds even if the child seeks only the pleasure of being held against the mother's body.) By interfering in the child's relationship to its mother the father arouses the child's hostility, and for the still unrepressed infant, this means a desire to do away with the interference altogether. The urge to destroy the father, however, cannot be consummated or even recognized, and so the psyche, to relieve the terrible dilemma, identifies itself with the Father image, creating a 'super-ego' as a new guide for the self (replacing the 'id' – the urges and desires which led to such a crisis). But what form does this super-ego take? Precisely that of the rules of society, traditionally learned under the father's guidance.

Trumps 3 and 4 of the Tarot represent the parents in their archetypal roles. But just as the Empress signified the natural world, so the Emperor carries the wider significance of the social world 'married' to nature. He symbolizes the laws of society, both good and bad, and the power that enforces them.

In ancient times, where the Goddess reigned, the king performed a special function. New life can only come from death; therefore, each winter, the Goddess's representatives sacrificed the old king, very often dismembering him and planting the pieces in the ground, thereby mystically fertilizing the earth. Later, when the male dominated religions took over, the king came to symbolize the rule of law which had clamped a lid of repression on what seemed to the patriarchs as the monstrous and chaotic darkness of the old order. We see this drama (much like Freud's substitution of super-ego for id) in many myths; such as Marduk, national hero of Babylon, killing Tiamat, the original mother of creation, because she is giving birth to monsters. Whether or not we see the old ways as monstrous or the new as civilized, the Emperor symbolizes the abstraction of society replacing the direct experience of nature.

In Rome, the concept of law versus chaos was carried to the point where stability, or 'law and order' to use the modern term, became virtues in themselves, apart from the inherent morality of those laws. No progress can be made in conditions of anarchy (runs the argument); bad laws need to be changed, but first the law must be obeyed at all costs. Any other approach can only destroy society. Today, we see this viewpoint embodied in an abstraction we call the 'system'. The Romans saw it more concretely in the personal figure of the Emperor, whom they described as the father of all his people.

In the Emperor's best aspect he indicates the stability of a just society that allows its members to pursue their personal needs and development. The natural world is chaotic; without some kind of social structure we could each spend all our lives fighting to survive. Society allows us both to work together and to benefit from the experience of those who lived before us.

Stability allows spiritual development as well. In many countries society supports the churches (though whether this arrangement furthers spirituality is arguable); in some Eastern countries monks are free to pursue their studies because laymen fill their beggar bowls. Without this social custom they would have to spend their time working to get bread.

In its more negative aspects the Emperor represents the power of unjust laws in a society where stability takes precedence over morality. Once we establish law and order as supreme then a corrupt ruler becomes a disaster. But if the entire system is corrupt, producing only bad rulers, then stability becomes the enemy of morality. The value of the symbol of the Emperor depends a very great deal on time and place. In an unjust society the Emperor's power hinders, rather than helps, personal development. A great many people have gone to gaol for attacking unjust laws.

Even at its best, however, the Emperor remains limited. Over the spontaneity of the Empress he has laid a network of repression. If we lose touch with our passions then life becomes cold and barren. The Rider pack Emperor (see fig. 5a) is drawn as old and stiff, dressed in iron, representing the sterility of a life rigidly governed by rules. The river which flowed so powerfully through the Empress's garden has here become a thin stream, barely able to penetrate a lifeless desert.

The card's other symbolism reflects its dual aspects. He holds an *ankh*, Egyptian symbol of life, to indicate that under the law he bears the power of life and death, and will hopefully use it well. Four rams, symbols of Aries, adorn his throne while at the crown's peak he bears the sign of Aries (unfortunately resembling a propellor). Now, Aries symbolizes force, aggression and war, but as the first sign of the zodiac it also signifies the new life of spring, which can emerge from the stability of a just society.

As the middle card of the first line of the Major Arcana the Emperor represents a crucial test. In the process of growing up it is indeed the rules of society that many people find most difficult to surmount. We must absorb these rules, as well as our society's traditions and beliefs, then go beyond them to find a personal code of conduct. This does not mean the attitude 'rules are made to be broken'. People who feel compelled to flaunt all laws remain as bound to those laws as the person who follows them blindly.

Because of the father's role in teaching us acceptably social behaviour, people who are trapped at the level of the Emperor are often people who have never really accepted the ordinary humanity of their father. They may recognize it rationally but it disturbs and haunts them. Similar problems plague those people for whom the Empress remains their mother's, rather than their own, passions and sensuality.

The idea of the Emperor as that of the limited values of social

structure arises mainly from Waite and his followers. The picture on
the right at the start of this section, from Paul Foster Case's Builders
of the Adytum (BOTA) deck drawn by Jessie Burns Parke, illustrates
another tradition. Here the Emperor symbolizes the sum total of
spiritual knowledge. He is drawn in profile (this is much more
common than the Rider pack full face image), linking them to the
Qabalist image for God as the 'Ancient of Days', a seated king in
profile. (The Ancient's face was never visible, only his crown with a
radiance beneath.)

The Emperor's arms and legs form an equilateral triangle over a
cross, the alchemical sign for fire. This figure is later reversed (in
Waite as well as Case) in the Hanged Man. As mentioned above, the
crossed legs are an esoteric sign, found also on the card of the World.
The BOTA Emperor sits on a cube rather than a throne. Also an
esoteric symbol, the cube symbolizes both the world and the Tarot
itself, as well as the Hebrew alphabet and the paths of the Tree of Life.
The symbolism arises from the fact that a cube contains twelve edges,
six faces, three axes, and of course a centre, adding up to twenty-two,
the number of trumps, Hebrew letters, and paths. And because the
Tree of Life is held to represent all creation the cube symbolizes the
universe.

In readings the Emperor indicates (following the Rider pack
image) the power of society, its laws and especially its authority to
enforce those laws. The appearance of the trump indicates an
encounter with the law. Again, the good or bad qualities depend on
the context.

More personally the Emperor can signify a time of stability and
order in a person's life, hopefully opening up creative energy. He also
can indicate a specific person who holds great power, either objective
or emotional, over the subject. This is very often the father, but it can
also be a husband or lover, especially for those people who treat their
lovers as substitute fathers to whom they surrender control of their
lives. I have seen readings so dominated by the Emperor that all of
life's possibilities become stunted and unfulfilled.

Like the Empress reversed, the Emperor, when upside down,
receives those elements complementary to his qualities when he is the
right way up. He is, in Waite's terms, 'benevolence and compassion';
new life in a stony desert. But the pendulum can swing too far. The
reversed Emperor can signify immaturity, and the inability to make
harsh decisions and carry them through.

(a)   *Figure 6*   (b)

The Hierophant

In most Tarot decks trump 5 is called either the Pope or the High Priest, terms which connect it by name as well as picture to trump 2, the archetype of inner truth. Waite wrote that he rejected 'Pope' because the title suggested a very specific example of the trump's general idea. The name 'Hierophant' belonged to the high priest of the Greek Eleusinian mysteries. Now, Waite describes his card as symbolizing the 'outer way' of churches and dogma. But his use of the mystery term suggests another interpretation, one more favoured by those who see the Tarot as a secret doctrine of occult practices rather than a more general embodiment of human patterns. This interpretation is dramatically portrayed in the picture of the Hierophant from Aleister Crowley's *Book of Thoth*, drawn by Frieda Harris. Here the trump signifies initiation into a secret doctrine, such as the various orders and lodges which flourished around the turn of the century and which have undergone a revival in England and America. The Order of the Golden Dawn, to which Waite and Crowley at one time both belonged, possibly originated the term 'Hierophant' for trump 5.

These two meanings, 'outer way' and 'secret doctrine', appear contradictory on the most elementary level. In reality they are very similar. Whether the two acolytes are being admitted to the Church or to an occult society, they are still entering a doctrine, with a set of beliefs which they must learn and accept before they can gain entrance. There is of course a fundamental difference between say, the catechism and the rituals of the Golden Dawn. For both, however, the trump indicates an education and a tradition. Therefore, if we see the first line as describing the development of the personality then the Hierophant, coming after the natural world and society, indicates the intellectual tradition of the person's particular society, and his or her education in that tradition.

Following Waite's interpretation (and thinking specifically of the Western pope) we can see the Hierophant as a companion to the Emperor. The word 'pope means 'father', and like the Roman Emperor the Pope is seen as a wise father guiding his children. Together, they share responsibility for humanity, the one providing physical needs, the other guiding spiritual growth. In one of the earliest treatises urging separation of Church and State, Dantë argued that the two functions must not be combined for fear of corruption. However, he never questioned the idea that the Church is responsible for our souls.

Today, many people do not understand the basic idea of a priesthood. Our democratic age rejects the notions of an intermediary between an individual and God. Note, however, that the Hierophant can also symbolize the 'dictatorship of the proletariat' or any other élite leading the masses where they cannot go themselves. Originally the special function of the priests was evident; they spoke to the gods through the oracles, an often terrifying practice, and most people quite happily let someone else do it for them. When Christianity rejected such graphic and immediate connection to God, the idea of the priest became, like the Emperor, more abstract. Basically it depends on the notion that most people do not really care much about God. The average person is happiest following worldly pursuits, money, family and politics. There are, however, certain people who, by temperament, feel very directly the spirit that runs through all our lives. Called to the priesthood by their own inner awareness, these people can speak to God for us. More important, they can speak to *us*, interpreting God's law so we may live proper lives, and eventually, after death, receive our reward of returning to God. After the resurrection we ourselves will dwell in sight of God. In life, however, we need the priests to guide us.

So runs the argument. Even if we agree with the principle, in practice it tends to break down. People become priests for all sorts of reasons – ambition, family pressure, etc. – while those who do feel a genuine calling to communicate with God may show very little talent for communicating with people. Moreover, like the social institutions of the Emperor, the religious institutions of the Hierophant can easily become corrupted by the authority given them, so that the priests see their power as an end in itself, prizing obedience above enlightenment. Obviously, the position of defending a doctrine will attract doctrinaire people.

Perhaps, however, we reject the idea of a guiding priesthood for a more subtle reason. Ever since the Reformation a notion that has gained greater and greater force in the West is that of the individual's ultimate responsibility for him or herself. The whole idea of an outer doctrine, a code of rules and beliefs accepted on faith, depends on the assumption that most people prefer to have someone else tell them what to do and think. This may very well be true. To really discover God inside yourself you must undergo some uncomfortable confrontations with your own psyche. Similarly, to decide for yourself what is the moral thing to do in all situations might require a constant agony of choice. Nevertheless, many people today simply cannot accept either society or a Church bearing the ultimate responsibility for their lives.

Perhaps the interpretation of the Hierophant as representing secret doctrines suits our age better. For then the doctrine does not tell us what to do, but instead gives us direction to begin working on ourselves. And the Tarot, as we saw with the Magician, sets itself against all Churches by leading us to personal salvation in this life. For Crowley the Hierophant represents initiation as the means through which the individual becomes united with the universe. The form and doctrine of the initiation change with each world age; having lasted nearly two thousand years, the current Piscean Age is coming to a close, so that the Hierophant is due to change, as will all strictly human relationships. Crowley comments that only the future can tell us what the new 'current of initiation' will be. But the basic quality of initiation as a merging with the cosmos always remains the same.

In the BOTA version of the Hierophant (as in the Rider pack) the crossed keys at the Hierophant's feet are gold and silver, representing the outer and inner ways, the sun and moon, the Magician and the High Priestess, which the doctrine teaches us to combine. In the Rider pack card both keys are gold, indicating that the dark side is hidden from those who follow the outer doctrine.

In the Waite-Smith imagery no veil blocks the entrance to the Church, as in the temple of the High Priestess. But the pillars are a dull grey. Those who enter here may receive protection from personal choice, but they will not pierce the secrets of duality. The unconscious remains closed. In many Tarot decks, the High

Priestess holds not a scroll but a small book, locked. And the keys of the Hierophant do not fit that tantalizing lock.

Still, we must not think that the outer doctrine of religion serves no purpose to the seeker. Like the general education, of which it is a particular example, it gives the individual a firm tradition in which to root his or her personal development. The modern Western phenomenon of a kind of eclectic mysticism, drawing inspiration from all religions, is an extremely unusual development. This is based, possibly, on global awareness plus the view of religion as a psychological state divorced from science and history. Thus we see religion as an experience rather than an explanation of the universe and accept that all religious experiences are valid, whatever contradictions they show on the surface. While this idea opens great possibilities, many people have noted its potential shallowness. The fact is, throughout the centuries, the great mystics have always spoken from deep within a tradition. The Qabalists were thoroughly Jewish, Thomas à Kempis a complete Christian, and the Sufis bowed to Mecca with all other orthodox Muslims. In its best aspect the Hierophant (as outer doctrine) can give us a place to start in creating a personal awareness of God.

One further aspect of the card's symbolism deserves special attention. The position of the three people (that is, a large figure presiding over two smaller ones on either side) introduces a motif that repeats itself, like the two pillars of the High Priestess, throughout the Major Arcana, and is resolved in Judgement and the world. The very next two cards after trump 5 repeat the motif, with the angel over the Lovers, and the charioteer of the Chariot over the black and white sphinxes.

We can see this trio as an emblem of the idea of a triad, such as the Christian trinity, or the triune picture of the mind: the id/ego/super-ego of Freud, or the unconscious/conscious/super-conscious of the three lines of the Major Arcana. To understand the meaning of the image we must return to the High Priestess. She sits between two pillars symbolizing the dualities of life. She herself signifies one side, the Magician the other. The Hierophant initiates two acolytes into his church. We see, therefore, that the Hierophant and the Lovers and the Chariot all represent attempts to mediate between the opposing poles of life and find some way, not to resolve them, but simply to hold them in balance. A religious doctrine, with its moral codes and explanations for life's most basic questions, does just that. If we surrender ourselves to a Church the contradictions of life all become answered; but not resolved.

In readings the card signifies Churches, doctrines, and education in general. Psychologically it can indicate orthodoxy, conformity to society's ideas and codes of behaviour, as well as, more subtly, a surrender of responsibility. The Emperor symbolized the rules themselves and their official enforcers; the Hierophant indicates our own inner sense of obedience. Reversed, the card means unorthodoxy, especially mental – forming original ideas. It can also, however, mean gullibility and this idea suggests another virtue of the card when it is the right way up. A society builds its intellectual tradition over hundreds of years. Those who accept that tradition receive from it a standard by which to judge new ideas and information. Those who reject it must find their own ways and can easily get lost in superficial ideas. There are many people who, having given up the dogma forced on them as children, fall into some new dogma, a cult or some extremist political group, just as rigid and perhaps more shallow. Having rejected tradition they have not really rejected the Hierophant. They have not accepted the responsibility of truly finding their own way.

(a) Figure 7 (b)

The Lovers

Of the various changes Arthur Waite and Pamela Smith made in traditional Tarot designs the card of the Lovers remains the most dramatic. Where the Tarot de Marseilles (on the right, above) shows a young man struck by Cupid's arrow and forced to choose between two women, the Rider pack shows a mature man and a single woman presided over by an angel. Further, while most decks indicate only a social situation; the Rider pack image clearly suggests the Garden of Eden, or rather, a new Garden of Eden, with the trees bringing enlightenment rather than the Fall.

The earlier version of trump 6 sometimes bears the title 'The Choice', and in divinatory readings means an important choice between two desires. Because one woman is fair and the other dark, a symbolism traditional in Europe where darkness always indicates evil and women in general indicate temptation, the choice was seen as between something respectable but perhaps dull, and something greatly desired but morally improper. The card can refer to a minor choice or even to a major crisis in a person's life. We see this ancient symbolism today in the various novels and films of middle-aged, middle class men tempted to give up their loved but rather boring wives for a younger 'wilder' woman.

The choice can, in fact, extend to a person's whole life. Even those people who never question the boundaries of their middle class respectability have made a choice as much as the life-long criminal. And there are many people who outwardly live socially acceptable lives yet inwardly fight constant torments of desire, fighting urges to adultery, or violence, or simply a desire to leave home and become a wandering tramp.

On the esoteric level the choice between the light and dark woman indicates the choice between the outer path (symbolized in the Rider pack by the Hierophant), where your life is laid out for you, and the inner path of the occultist, which can lead to a confrontation with your hidden desires. The Church labelled magicians as devil worshippers, and in Christian allegories the dark woman usually stood for Satan.

These meanings all see the choice between light and dark in the widest possible terms. In the context of the first line of trumps we can see it in a much more specific way, that of the first real choice a person makes independently of his or her parents. Until the sexual urge rouses itself most people are content to act out their parents' expectations for them. The sexual urge, however, points us where *it* wants to go. As a result we begin to break away in other areas as well. It is very rare that the partners our parents would choose for us are the ones we would choose for ourselves. If the difference is too extreme, or the parents too controlling, then the person can face a painful choice.

Paul Douglas has commented that the darkhaired woman, who appears much older, is the boy's mother, and the choice is whether to stay under her protection or strike out on his own. Those who believe, with Freud, that a boy's first desire is directed towards his mother will see here a classic Oedipal dilemma. One part of the personality wishes to maintain the hidden fantasy life of a union with the mother, while another wishes to find a true love in the reality of the boy's own generation. But we do not have to accept the Freudian doctrine to see the wider implications of this choice. Whether or not the boy secretly desires his mother the life lived under the parents' protection is safe and comfortable. But he (or she, for girls basically face the same questions, though sometimes in different forms) can never become a true individual without making a break. And nothing indicates this more strongly than sexuality.

Therefore, the traditional version of trump 6 represents adolescence. Not only does sexuality emerge at this time but also intellectual and moral independence. Cards 3, 4, and 5 represented us as shaped by the great forces of nature, society, and parents. In card 6 the individual emerges, a true personality with its own ideas and purposes, able to make important choices based, not on parental orders, but on its own assessment of desires and responsibilities.

These meanings belong to the card's traditional structure. In designing his own version of the Lovers Waite addressed a different question. What functions do sex and love ultimately serve in a person's life? And what deep meanings can we find in the powerful drama of two people joining their hearts and bodies? Waite called his picture, 'the card of human love, here exhibited as part of the way, the truth, and the life'.

The sexual drive leads us away from isolation. It pushes us to form vital relationships with other people, and finally opens the way to love. Through love we not only achieve a unity with someone else, but we are given a glimpse of the greater meanings and deeper significance of life. In love we give up part of that ego control which isolates us not only from other people but from life itself. Therefore the angel appears above the man's and woman's heads, a vision unobtainable to each person individually, but glimpsed by both of them together.

Religion, philosophy, and art have always seized on the symbolism of male and female as representing duality. We have already seen this idea reflected in the Magician and the High Priestess, as well as the Empress and the Emperor. The symbolism here is reinforced by the fact that the Tree of Life, with its Magician like flames, stands behind the man, while the Tree of Knowledge, entwined with the serpent (symbol not of evil but of unconscious wisdom) stands behind the woman. The angel unites these two principles. In traditional teachings men and women are held to contain, within their bodies, separate life principles. Through physical love these principles join together.

Occultists, however, have always recognized both these elements within the self. Today we hear many people say that everyone contains both male and female qualities; usually, however, they are referring to vague ideas of social behaviour, such as aggression and gentleness. When male and female were seen as opposite in their deepest natures the occultist view was much more radical. One way of describing the goal of the Major Arcana is to say it brings out and unites the male and female principles. Therefore, in many decks, the dancer in the World is an hermaphrodite.

According to Qabalists and Hermetic philosophers all humanity (and indeed, even the Deity) was originally hermaphroditic; male and female became separated only as a consequence of the Fall. Thus, on the outer level, each of us is only half a person and only through love can we find a sense of unity.

We find this same idea in Plato, but with an interesting variation. One of the Platonic myths states that humans were originally double creatures, but of three kinds: male-female, male-male, and female-female. Believing that humans possessed too much power Zeus split them with a thunderbolt, and now each one of us is looking for his or her other half. In contrast to the Jewish and Christian myths Plato's story gives equal reality to homosexuals. It reminds us of the danger in the too easy symbolism of male and female as ultimate opposites. The Magician and the High Priestess are mixed very subtly in each of us. And the angel can be evoked by any two lovers. It is not the roles that matter, but the reality of the union.

In the usual Christian interpretation of Genesis Eve bears the greater guilt, not only because she ate first, but because her sensuality tempted Adam to fall. Man supposedly was ruled by reason and woman by desire. This split led some Christians to declare that women had no souls. The whole myth of the Fall, however, with its emphasis on disobedience and punishment, is really meant to serve a repressive morality. Physical passions were seen as dangerous to society and therefore had to be controlled. As Joseph Campbell points out in *The Masks of God* the ancient goddess religion of Palestine contained the same drama of a serpent, a Tree of Life, and an apple. But in the old story the initiate was given the apple by the goddess to allow him to enter paradise, rather than it being the cause of his expulsion. The ancient Hebrews reversed the myth, partly as a way of branding the old religion as evil, but also because they, like the Babylonians, considered the old ways 'monstrous'.

The Tarot, however, is a path of liberation. The fear that Jahweh expresses, that human beings 'will become like us', is precisely the Tarot's purpose – to fully bring out the divine spark in us and unite it with our conscious selves, to end the duality of God and human and make them one. Therefore, though it keeps much of the same symbolism as Genesis, the Rider pack Lovers subtly reverses the meaning.

Notice that while the man looks at the woman the woman looks at the angel. If the male is indeed reason, then rationality can only reach beyond its limits through the medium of passion. By its nature reason controls and contains, while passion tends to break down all limits. Our tradition has set the body and the rational mind at odds with each other. The Tarot teaches us that we must unite them (a single mountain rises between the two lovers) and that it is not the controlling power of reason that raises the senses to a higher level, but, rather, the other way around.

We can see this in direct psychological terms. Most people are bound within their egos or the masks they present to the world. But if they can surrender to sexual passion, they can, at least for a moment, transcend their isolation. Those who cannot release their egos, even for an instant, misuse sex, and are misused by it. Sex becomes a means of gaining power over someone else, but it never satisfies. When a person rejects the body's desire to release itself with another person the result is depression. The angel has been denied.

At the same time the passions alone cannot bring us to the angel. They need to be guided by the reason as much as the reason needs the passions to set it free. Those who simply go wherever their desires lead them are often thrown from one experience to another.

Paul Foster Case names the angel as Raphael, who presides over the super-conscious. This brings us back to the triune mind; here we learn that the three levels of the mind are not separate and isolated, like the three stories of a house, but that the super-conscious is actually a product of the conscious and unconscious joined together. The pathway lies through the unconscious because that is where we find the true energy of life. In fact, the super-conscious can be described as the energy of the unconscious brought out and transformed to a higher state. Part of that transformation lies in consciousness giving the energy form, direction, and meaning.

If in the triangular motif the two figures below represent the dualities of life, while the larger figure above symbolizes a mediating force between them, then in trump 6 the mediator is sexual love. When we surrender to it we experience a glimpse of something greater than ourselves. Only a glimpse, and only for a moment; true liberation requires finally a great deal more than passion. But love can help us see the path, and know a little of the joy that waits for us at the end of it. A number of mystics, notably Saint Teresa, have described union with God in terms of sexual ecstasy.

The divinatory meanings for the Waite-Smith image are straightforward. They refer to the importance of love in a person's life and to a specific lover; very often to marriage or a long relationship. The card implies that the particular relationship has been or will prove to be very valuable to the person, leading him or her to a new understanding of life. If some specific problem is being considered in the reading then the Lovers indicates help in some way, either practically through the lover's assistance, or through emotional support. But this is not always true. The Lovers, in the position of the past, especially in relation to cards indicating a refusal to look at the present situation, can indicate a crippling nostalgia for a past love.

The earlier cards all represented archetypes. When we reversed them we added the missing elements. But here the individual has advanced and now the reversed meaning shows weakness and blocks. It is first of all a destructive love, particularly in a bad marriage. It can refer to romantic or sexual problems that dominate a person's life, either from difficulties with a specific person, or because the person finds love simply a great problem. Because the Waite-Smith picture indicates a mature love, and the traditional image shows the process of adolescent choice, either version reversed indicates romantic immaturity; the prolonged adolescence that keeps some people involved in childish fantasies long after their bodies have fully matured.

Figure 8

The Chariot

The earlier versions of this card, which showed the Chariot pulled by two horses rather than two sphinxes, derives from a number of historical and mythological sources. Primarily it comes out of the processions given in Rome and other places for a conquering hero, when his chariot carried him through the streets that were filled with cheering citizens. The custom apparently answers some deep psychic need for group participation. We still practice it today, two thousand years later, in the parades given to presidents, generals, and astronauts, with open limousines replacing the chariot.

The Chariot implies more than a greater victory. To drive a two horse vehicle at speed requires total control over the animals; the activity serves as a perfect vehicle for the powerful will. Plato, in the *Phaedrus*, refers to the mind as a chariot drawn by a black and white horse, the exact image of the Tarot.

A certain Hindu myth tells of Shiva destroying a triple city of the demons. To do so he requires that all creation be subordinated to his will. The gods make a chariot for Shiva, using not only themselves but the heavens and the Earth as materials. The sun and moon become the wheels and the winds the horses. (The symbol on the front of the Tarot Chariot, like a nut and bolt, or a wheel and axle, is called the lingam and yoni, standing for Shiva, the masculine principle, and Parvati, the feminine principle, united in a single figure.) Through the myth's images we learn that spiritual victory over evil comes when we can focus all of nature, as well as the unconscious energy embodied in Shiva himself, through the conscious will.

These two fables show two different aspects of the idea of will. The story of Shiva speaks of a true victory, in which the spirit has found a focus to release its total force. But the *Phaedrus* gives us an image of the triumphant ego, which controls rather than resolves the basic conflicts of life. Those Tarot commentators who see the cards as a group of separate images, each one contributing some vital lesson to our spiritual understanding, tend to give the Chariot its wider meaning. They point out that the Qabalistic title for the number 7, with all its mystic connotations, is 'Victory'.

In many places, particularly India, the horse became associated with death and funerals. When the rising patriarchy abolished the ritual sacrifice of the king, a horse was killed instead. The horse sacrifice became the most holy, associated with immortality. Even today, horses are used to pull the coffins of great leaders. (A bizarre junction of two aspects of the Chariot was seen in the death of John Kennedy. He was killed in his limousine during a parade, and then a horse – who rebelled against his trainer's control – pulled his coffin in the state funeral.) These connections suggest the idea of the soul's victory over mortality.

When we look at the cards sequentially we see that 7 is only the victory of the first line of the Major Arcana. It crowns that line's process of maturation, but by necessity it cannot address the great areas of the unconscious and super-conscious. Seen this way the Chariot shows us the developed ego; the lessons of the early cards have been absorbed, the adolescent period of searching and self-creation has been passed, and now we see the mature adult, successful in life, admired by others, confident and content with himself, able to control feelings, and above all, to direct the will.

Like the Magician the Charioteer carries a magic wand. Unlike the Magician he does not raise it above his head to heaven. His power is subordinate to his will. His hands hold no reins. His strong character alone controls the opposing forces in life.

The lingam and yoni indicate his mature sexuality which is under his control. Thus he is not the victim of his emotions and his sexuality contributes to a satisfying life. The glowing square on his chest, a symbol of vibrant nature, links him to the sensual world of the Empress, but the eight pointed star on his crown shows his mental energy directing his passions (symbolists consider the eight pointed star as halfway between the square of the material world and the circle of the spiritual). His chariot looms larger than the town behind indicating that his will is more powerful than the rules of society. However, the fact that his chariot is not in motion indicates that he is not a rebel. The wheels of the chariot rest on water, showing that he draws energy from the unconscious, though the chariot itself, resting on land, separates him from a direct contact with that great force.

We have mentioned the sexual symbolism of the lingam and yoni. While Hindu myth connects horses to death, Freudian dream symbolism connects them to the sexual energy of the libido. By controlling the horses (or sphinxes) the Charioteer controls his instinctive desires.

Various magic signs adorn his body. His skirt bears symbols of ceremonial magic, his belt shows the sign and planets. The two lunar faces on his shoulders are named 'Urin and Thummim', the supposed shoulder plates of the High Priest in Jerusalem and which therefore suggest the Hierophant. At the same time the lunar plates refer to the High Priestess. Note also that the cloth at the back of the chariot suggests the High Priestess's veil; he has set the mystery of the unconscious behind him.

We see, therefore, in the Chariot's symbolism all the previous cards of the first line. The wand and symbols indicate the Magician, the water, sphinxes, and veil symbolize the High Priestess, the square and green earth symbolize the Empress, the city symbolizes the Emperor, the shoulder plates symbolize the Hierophant, and the lingam and yoni symbolize the Lovers. All these forces contribute to the outer personality.

And yet – observe the Chariot with its stone-like qualities. Observe the charioteer himself merging into his stone vehicle. The mind that subordinates all things to conscious will runs the risk of becoming rigid, cut off from the very forces it has learned to control. Observe also that the black and white sphinxes are not reconciled to each other. They look in opposite directions. The charioteer's will holds them together in a tense balance. If that will should fail, the Chariot and its rider will be torn apart.

Paul Douglas has compared the Chariot to Jung's idea of the 'persona'. As we grow up we create a kind of mask to deal with the outside world. If we have dealt successfully with the various challenges of life, then the different aspects symbolized by the other cards will become integrated into this ego-mask. But we can too easily confuse this successful persona with the true self, even to the point that if we try to discard the mask we will fear its loss as a kind of death. This is why the second line of the Major Arcana, which deals precisely with the release of the self from its outer masks, bears Death as its next to last card.

So far we have considered the Chariot as an emblem of personal maturity. But the idea of human will extends beyond the individual. With its images of the mind subduing and utilizing the forces of life the Chariot is a perfect symbol for civilization, which creates order out of the chaos of nature by using the natural world as the raw materials for its agriculture and cities. One of the chief Qabalistic connotations for the card extends this idea. By its connection with the Hebrew letter 'Iain' the Chariot carries the quality of 'speech'. Speech has always seemed to humans to represent the rational mind and its dominance over nature. As far as we know only humans possess language (though chimpanzees have shown themselves capable of learning human sign language, and whales and dolphins may possess developed languages of their own) and we may say that speech separates us from the animal. Adam gained control over the beasts in Eden by speaking their names. Most important, humans use language to transmit the information that allows civilization to continue.

However, just as the ego is limited, so is speech. First of all, speech restricts our experience of reality. By forming a description of the world, by giving everything a label, we erect a barrier between ourselves and experience. When we look at a tree, we do not feel the impact of a living organism; rather, we think 'tree' and move on. The label has replaced the thing itself. Also, by relying too much on this rational quality of language we ignore experiences that cannot be expressed in words. We have already seen how the High Priestess signifies intuitive wisdom beyond language. Certain experiences, especially mystical union with spirit, cannot be described. Language can only hint at them with metaphors and fables. People who rely totally on speech have even gone so far as to insist that non-verbal experiences, or experiences which cannot be measured by psychological tests, do not exist. This is simply because they cannot be scientifically described. Such dogmatism receives its perfect symbol in the charioteer's merging with his stone wagon.

So far we have considered every symbol in the picture except, perhaps, the most obvious one: the two sphinxes. Waite borrowed this innovation from Eliphas Lévi, the great pioneer of Qabalistic Tarot. Like the two pillars of the High Priestess, or the black and white horses they replace, the sphinxes signify the dualities and contradictions of life. Once again, we see the triangular motif. Here the mediating force is will-power.

The use of sphinxes instead of horses suggests several deeper meanings. The sphinx in Greek legend was a riddler, presenting the mystery of life to the people of Thebes. The myth tells us that the sphinx siezed the young men of the city and asked them the following riddle: 'What creature walks on four legs in the morning, two legs at noon, and three legs in the evening?' Those who could not answer were devoured. Now, the answer is 'man' who crawls as a baby, walks upright as an adult, and uses a cane in old age. The implication is clear. If you do not understand your basic humanity, with its strengths and weaknesses, then life will destroy you. The Chariot symbolizes maturity, accepting the limits of life, plus the faculty of speech, that is, rational understanding, which is used to define existence and therefore to control it.

But a further meaning lurks here. The man who answered the sphinx's riddle was Oedipus, who arrived in Thebes after killing his father. Freud's emphasis on incest has diverted attention from the deeper message of the Oedipus story. Oedipus was the perfect image of the successful man. Not only did he save Thebes from a menace and become king of the city but he did so by his understanding of life. He knew what man was. Yet he did not know himself. His own inner reality remained closed to him until the gods forced him to confront it. And the gods *did* force him. If the oracles had not spoken first to his father and then to him, Oedipus would never have done the things he did. Therefore, though he understood the outer meaning of man's life he did not understand either who he really was, or his relation to the gods who controlled his life. And these two subjects are precisely the concerns of the second and third lines of the Major Arcana. In the second we go beyond the ego to find the true self. In the third we deal openly with the archetypal forces of existence and reach at last a full integration of those dualities which the charioteer was able to dominate but never reconcile.

The divinatory meanings of the Chariot derive from its powerful will. In a reading the card signifies that the person is successfully controlling some situation through the force of his or her personality. The card implies that a situation contains some contradictions and that these have not been brought together but simply held under control. This is not to stress too highly the negative undertones of the card. When it is the right way up the Chariot basically means success; the personality in charge of the world around it. If it appears as the outcome in a reading dealing with problems then it indicates victory.

Reversed, the card's inherent contradictions gain greater force. The Chariot upside down implies that the approach of will-power has proven unsuccessful, and the situation has got out of control. Unless the person can find some other approach to the difficulties, he or she faces disaster. Will-power alone cannot always sustain us. Like Oedipus we must sometimes learn to give way to the gods.

Chapter 5.

Turning Inwards

The Search for Self-knowledge

ith the second line of the Major Arcana we move from the outer world and its challenges to the inner self. The contradictions concealed in the Chariot's powerful image must now be faced openly. The mask of ego must die.

Dramatic as it sounds this situation is actually very common, at least in the need if not the fulfilment. Self-questioning and searching have long been seen as features of middle age. When people are young they are concerned mainly with victory over the forces of life, finding a partner and achieving success. When success has been found, however, people may wonder about the value of it. The question, 'Who am I beneath all my possessions, beneath all the images I present to other people?' takes on more and more importance. Today, many younger people are not waiting for middle-age and success to ask these things. A characteristic of our time is the desire for life to have a sense of meaning, of inner essence. And more and more people are deciding that the first place to look for such meaning is within themselves.

This idea, in fact, is only a half-truth. The Magician teaches us that, as physical beings, we find reality only in connection with the outer world; the inner truth of the High Priestess is a potential and must be manifested through the consciousness of the Magician. But as long as our masks and habits and defences close us off from self-knowledge so that we never know *why* we act, then all the things we do remain meaningless. The flow between the Magician and the High Priestess needs to be free for life to possess value.

Because the line basically reverses the emphasis of the first seven cards, many of the cards appear as mirror images to the ones above them. The sexual polarity of trumps 1 and 2 become turned around in Strength and the Hermit, while the principle of light and dark, outer and inner, remain in the same positions. The Wheel of Fortune turns away from the natural and mindless world of the Empress to a vision of inner mysteries. At the end of the line Temperance shows us a new kind of victory. The Chariot's force has been replaced by balance and calm. Where the charioteer's stone chariot removed him from direct contact with the earth and the river, the angel of Temperance stands with one foot on land, one in water, showing the personality in harmony with itself and life.

Another theme appears in the second line. So far the cards have presented a series of lessons to us, things we must learn about life to become mature and successful in the outer world. But enlightenment is a deeply personal experience. It cannot be studied or even pondered but only lived. The series of outer lessons culminate in the Wheel of Fortune which shows us a vision of the world and ourselves which must be answered. The Hanged Man, however, shows something else entirely. Here we see, not a lesson, but the image of enlightenment itself, the outer personality turned upside down by a very real and personal experience.

In between these two cards, and at the exact centre of the whole Major Arcana, lies Justice, carefully balancing the scales between inner and outer, past and future, rationality and intuition, knowledge and experience.

Figure 9

Strength

Waite's change of the Lovers was the most obvious of his Tarot alterations; his switch of Strength with Justice remains the most controversial. He himself gives no real reason for the change. 'For reasons which satisfy myself, this card has been interchanged with that of Justice, which is usually numbered eight. As the variation carries nothing which will signify to the reader there is no cause for explanation.' The reasons are certainly more than personal. Not only Waite but Paul Foster Case and Aleister Crowley placed Strength as 8 and Justice as 11. Probably they all followed the Order of the Golden Dawn, whose secret Tarot deck also switched the two cards.

This connection to a secret order suggests the idea of initiation. Now, the Golden Dawn, of course, did not originate the practice of initiation, though it claimed to receive its specific rituals directly from spirit instructors. Initiation goes back thousands of years and is seen all over the world, from Egyptian temples to the Australian desert. It represents a special means of psychological transformation – the very subject of the Tarot's middle line. By referring Justice and the cards around it to this ancient idea we gain a wider understanding of the Tarot as an experience.

It is worth considering the implications of the old arrangement of trumps. The image of Justice suggests weighing your life in the balance. The second line takes us away from the outer achievements of the first and into the self. Thus Justice in the first position would mean an assessment of what your life has meant to you, followed by a decision to search inward for greater meaning. Obviously, this fits very nicely. But if Justice comes first then all these things occur rationally; the assessment arises as a conscious reaction to dissatisfaction. How much more powerful this assessment appears when it arises from within, forced on us by the powerful vision of the Wheel of Fortune. The double-edged sword of Justice implies action, a response to the knowledge gained in the assessment. The idea of response leads directly to the Hanged Man. If Justice came first then the Hermit would follow it. As a seeker of wisdom the Hermit would also represent a valid response to Justice. But again, if we allow that wisdom to come before Justice, then the Hanged Man shows a response from deep inside.

Now consider Strength in both places. The picture shows a woman taming a lion. Briefly, the image suggests the energy of the unconscious released and calmed, 'tamed' by the direction of conscious understanding. Such an idea would easily belong in the middle position. We would then describe the card as the central test of the whole line. And certainly the peacefulness and great reversal of the Hanged Man would follow Strength perfectly.

But we can also see Strength as the qualities vital for beginning the line. The search inward cannot be accomplished by the ego. We need to confront feelings and desires long hidden from our conscious thoughts. If we attempt to transform ourselves by a wholly rational process we create another kind of persona. Something very like this in fact happens quite often. Many people feel a lack of spontaneity in their lives. They look around them or read books on psychology, and observe, with a certain jealousy, or even shame at their own repressions, the characteristics of spontaneous people. And then, rather than follow the fearful process of releasing their hidden fears and desires, they carefully imitate spontaneity. They have extended the Chariot to a new domain.

By making Strength number 8 we set it against the Chariot, as a different kind of power, not the ego's will, but the inner Strength to confront yourself calmly and without fear. The mysteries can be brought out because we have found the Strength to face them. The lion signifies all the feelings, fears, desires, and confusions suppressed by the ego in its attempt to control life. The charioteer drew upon his inner feelings as a source of energy, but was always careful to direct that energy where he consciously decided it should go. Strength allows the inner passions to emerge, as the first step in going beyond the ego.

On a very simple level we can see this emergence of suppressed feelings in the person who allows him or herself to act 'childishly', to weep or scream; in short, to do all those things that previously seemed foolish or embarrassing. On a deeper level the lion symbolizes the whole force of personality, usually smoothed over by the demands of civilized life. Strength releases this energy in order to use it as a kind of fuel, propelling us along the inner path of the Hermit. This purpose can only be accomplished because the lion is 'tamed' at the same time that it is released. Strength opens up the personality like Pandora opening her box. It does so, however, with a sense of peace, a love of life itself, and a great confidence in the final result. Unless we truly believe that the process of self-discovery is a joyous one we will never follow it through.

The symbolism of the pictures and numbers reinforces the comparison of Strength and the Chariot. The Chariot shows a man and Strength shows a woman. Traditionally, of course, these represent rationality and emotion, aggression and surrender. Also traditionally, the Chariot's number 7 belongs to 'male' magic, the number 8 to 'female'. This symbolism arises from anatomy. The male body contains seven openings (counting the nose as one), the female eight. Also, the male body possesses seven points, the arms and legs, the head, the centre, and the penis. The female possesses eight, the breasts replacing the penis.

What do we mean by male and female magic? Esoteric theory considers sexual energy as a manifestation of the energy principles underlying the entire universe; male and female being similar to the positive and negative poles of electro-magnetism. Through manipulation of this bipolar energy, 'magic' power results. The occultist considers these principles a science, no more, and no less, mysterious than the modern scientist's manipulation of atomic energy. We can describe the Rider pack Lovers as a schematic energy diagram. Therefore, the Chariot and Strength belong together esoterically as the practical manifestation of the principles symbolized in the Magician and the High Priestess.

Psychologically they also embody two kinds of power. Our society emphasizes the 'masculine' force of control; conquest, dominating the world through reason and will. But the 'feminine' qualities of intuition and spontaneous emotion are far from weakness. To release your deepest emotions with love and faith requires great courage as well as strength.

The Fool comes in here. Only by a kind of psychic leap can we move from the conscious to the unconscious. And only a fool would make such a jump, for why give up success, control? The gods forced Oedipus; what inner needs will force the rest of us?

Strength's position, as first in the line, links the card to the Magician, as does the infinity sign, another reference to 8, above her head. The reversal of sex indicates a joining of aspects from both the male and female archetypes. The Magician's active involvement with life has been modified by the inner peace implied in the High Priestess.

The woman's sensual figure, her blonde hair, and the flower belt linking her to the lion, connect the card to the Empress as well. The Empress represents natural instincts and passion; again we see the image of emotional energy, the 'animal desires' as some Tarot commentators call it, released and tamed. Waite describes the flower belt as a second infinity sign, with one loop around the woman's waist, the other around the lion's neck. We can describe Strength as the Magician united with the Empress; that is, the Magician's power of consciousness and direction has mingled with the Empress's sensuality, giving it a sense of purpose and leading to the Hermit. Notice that for the first line 1 plus 3 equals 4, the Emperor. For the second line 1 plus 3 becomes multiplied by 2; the inner truth of the High Priestess.

Another aspect of the trump carries this unity of 1 and 3 still further. The Hebrew letter given by Case and others to Strength is Teth. Teth refers Qabalistically to 'snake'; but the Hebrew for snake also means 'magic'. All over the world people have made this connection; from the snakes on Hermes's magic wand to the kundalini power of Tantric occultism in India and Tibet. And the snake, in kundalini and elsewhere, stands for sexuality. The Tarot, as we know from the serpent twined around the Tree of Life behind the woman on the Lovers, considers sexuality to be a force towards enlightenment. If, esoterically, Strength stands for the actual practice of sexual magic, psychologically it refers again to releasing that energy bound up in our strongest feelings. When we compare Strength with the Devil we will see that the release here is actually a partial one. The lion is controlled and directed rather than allowed to take the self wherever it wants to go.

In alchemy the lion stands for gold, the sun, and sulphur. Sulphur is a lower element and gold (in alchemy) the highest. The process by which sulphur becomes gold is precisely the process of transforming the lower self. And the design of Temperance, the last card of the line, with its liquid poured from one cup to another, depicts the alchemical goal of blending the opposites into a new and more meaningful existence.

Those who find life a matter of strict control, who see the unconscious as a 'moral sewer' of repressions (as Jung characterized the narrow Freudian view), and find the passions a torment, will see the lion as natural forces which the rational mind must overcome. Some older Tarot decks, including the Visconti, showed Heracles killing the Nemean lion. The passions conquered by reason. But the lion also stood for Christ, the radiant power of God. Those who allow the unconscious energy within themselves to emerge, guiding it with love and a faith in life, will discover that the energy is not a destructive beast but the same spirit force drawn down through the lightning rod of the Magician.

In readings the card of Strength indicates the ability to face life, and particularly some difficult problem or time of change, with hope and eagerness. It shows a person strong from within, experiencing life passionately yet peacefully, without being controlled or carried away by those passions. The card represents the finding of the strength to begin or continue some difficult project, despite fear and emotional strain.

If Strength appears in connection with the Chariot it can signify an alternative to force and will-power, especially, of course, if the Chariot is reversed. The two cards can also symbolize complementary sides, the best configuration being Strength in the position of the inner self, and the Chariot in the position of the outer (the vertical and horizontal lines of a cross). Then we see a person who acts powerfully but with a sense of calm.

Strength reversed indicates first of all weakness. The courage to face life fails and the person feels overwhelmed and pessimistic. It signifies also a torment from within. The bestial side of the lion breaks away from the unity of spirit and sensuality. The passions become the enemy, threatening to destroy the conscious personality and the life it has built up for itself.

Figure 10

The Hermit

Like the six-pointed star within the Hermit's lantern, the idea of the Hermit goes in two directions; one inner, one outer. Primarily the card means a withdrawal from the outer world for the purpose of activating the unconscious mind. We see this process symbolized in the downward pointing 'water' triangle, as the alchemists called it. But the Hermit also signifies a teacher who will show us how to begin this process, and will help us find our way. The upward pointing 'fire' triangle symbolizes this special guide, who might be an occult teacher, a therapist, our own dreams, or even a spirit guide evoked from within the self.

The image of the Hermit occupied a special place in the medieval imagination. Living in the woods or the desert, totally withdrawn from all the normal concerns of humanity, the hermit presented an alternative to the Church. The European version of a yogi ascetic, he demonstrated the possibility of approaching God through personal experience. People often looked upon the hermits as living saints, and attributed magic powers to them, in the way that yoga disciples will tell wonderful stories about their masters.

Though the hermit withdrew from society he or she[1] did not

[1] Women often became hermits and the medieval hatred of women sometimes became a veneration of a particular woman who had supposedly conquered the evil of her sex.

withdraw from humanity. Among other functions, they gave shelter and sometimes blessings to travellers. Countless stories, especially the Grail legends, depict the hermit who acts as a giver of wisdom to the knight on a spiritual quest. Again, we see the Hermit's double image: example and guide.

The Hermit image has persisted long after the special practice has died away. The transcendental philosopher Ralph Waldo Emerson travelled days through remote Scotland to find the cabin of Thomas Carlyle. Emerson's friend, Henry David Thoreau, himself lived in a cabin at Walden Pond to find a sense of himself and of nature. He then wrote about it as an example to others. Nietzsche's *Dus Sprach Zarathustra* enshrined the Hermit's image; the book begins with Zarathustra's return after achieving personal transformation. And today, countless people have given themselves to Eastern gurus in the hope that these hermit-like teachers can transform their lives.

For those who cannot find an actual guide the psyche will often provide one. Jung and his followers have described their patients many dreams of wise old men guiding them on mysterious journeys into the psyche. In many cases dream analysis discovered that the dream guide actually stood for the therapist. The unconscious can recognize a Hermit teacher before the conscious mind can.

The great thirteenth century Qabalist, Abraham Abulafia described three levels of Qabalah. The first was doctrine; that which can be learned from texts. The second came from the direct guidance given by a personal teacher, while the third, the most developed, was the direct experience of ecstatic union with God. These three levels connect very directly to the Tarot, not only in the three lines, but in three specific trumps which together form an isosceles triangle. The first level we see in the Hierophant; the third directly below the Hierophant, one level removed, appears in the joyous child of card 19, the Sun. The second level, however, comes not in the card between them, the Hanged Man, but on the other end of the pattern, as the second card in the second line, the Hermit.

Doctrine and mystery both come as the end of a process; doctrine because you first must arrange your life before you can approach the study of a special way (Qabalists often restricted certain important texts to people over thirty-five), and ecstasy because you first must pass the archetypal confrontation with darkness and mystery. A guide, however, appears at the very start of the journey, after the traveller has found the Strength to begin.

As an emblem of personal development, rather than a guide, the Hermit signifies the idea that only by withdrawing from the outer world can we awaken the inner self. Those who see the Tarot in two halves, with the Wheel of Fortune as the mid-point, view the Hermit as the period of contemplation before the Wheel of Life turns towards its second half. When we view the Tarot in lines of seven we see that this withdrawal, and the vision of the Wheel itself, are steps towards a greater goal.

We see the Hermit on a cold lonely peak. He has left the world of the senses to enter the mind. This image of the mind as stark and chill conveys only a partial truth, or rather, an illusion. The mind is rich with symbols, with joy, with the light and love of the spirit. But before we can apprehend these things we must first experience the mind as a silent alternative to the noisy world of the senses. For shamans the barren peak is often a direct reality. In places as far apart as Siberia and the American South-West shaman candidates go alone into the wilderness to seek the spirit guides who will teach them how to heal.

The Hermit signifies a transition. Through the techniques of meditation, or psychic discipline, or analysis, we allow the hidden parts of the psyche to begin to speak to us. Later we will experience a sense of rebirth, first as an angel (the eternal part of the self, beyond the ego), then later, more deeply felt, as a free child riding forth from the garden of past experience. For now, the path belongs to the image of the wise old man, alone, supported and warmed by his stiff grey cloak of contemplation.

The symbol of the lantern returns us to the Hermit as guide and teacher. He tolds the light out to us, indicating his willingness to lead us and our ability to find the way if we will only use the Strength we have to follow. In some decks the Hermit conceals his lantern under his cloak, and then it symbolizes the light of the unconscious hidden under the cloak of the conscious mind. By making it visible, yet within a lantern, the Rider pack indicates that we release the light through a definite process of self-awareness, and that this process is available to anyone.

We have seen the star both as a symbol of the Hermit as teacher, and also as a light of the unconscious, beckoning us to discover its secrets. It further signifies the goal of resolving the opposites of life. The water and fire triangles traditionally represent not only two elements usually opposed, but also male and female united in a single form.

The Hermit's staff suggests a wizard's staff, and therefore the magic wand of the Magician. Whereas the Fool used the wand instinctively, the Hermit leans on it as a conscious support. It therefore symbolizes the teaching which helps open the inner awareness.

Directly below the High Priestess the Hermit relates to her principle of withdrawal, indicating again that we must in some sense leave the outer world if we wish to work on ourselves. As with Strength the second line reverses the sexual archetype. The role symbolism here teaches us that a deliberate mental effort, based on specific techniques and teachings, takes us beyond the locked up intuition of the High Priestess's closed temple. The waters of that temple are not fully released; the veil remains in place until the lightning of the Tower, below the Hermit, tears it open. Under the influence of trump 9, however, the unconscious speaks to us from behind the veil, through symbols, dreams, and visions.

The distinction between male-female symbolism and the reality of individual people leads us to some important realizations about archetypes. We tend to see hermits and teachers as wise old *men*, even in our dreams, because our two thousand year old patriarchy has so impressed this image on our minds. In earlier times, the guides were most often women, as representatives of the Great Goddess, and even in our age such women as Madame Blavatsky have served this ancient function. The fact that our dreams often choose wise old men demonstrates the very important fact that the unconscious too draws its material from the cultural background of the individual dreamer. Many people view archetypes as rigid fixed images shared by all people at all times. Rather, archetypes are tendencies for the mind to form certain *kinds* of images, such as that of a guide, and the specific form an image takes will depend very much on a person's cultural background and experience. Medieval Grail initiations and Australian desert rites follow the same archetypal pattern; it underlies them like a grid. Yet the outer form of that pattern varies immensely.

The divinatory meanings for the Hermit derive from both its aspects. On the one hand it symbolizes a withdrawal from outer concerns. The person may physically remove himself, but this is not really necessary. What matters is the inner transfer of attention from 'getting and spending' as Wordsworth called our worldly activities, to a person's inner needs. It therefore requires an emotional withdrawal from other people and from activities once thought to be all-important. The card carries within it a sense of deliberate purpose, of withdrawing to work on self-development. In connection with this sense of purpose and with the picture of an old man the card symbolizes maturity, and a knowledge of what really matters in a person's life.

The card can also signify assistance from a definite guide, sometimes, as indicated above, a psychic guide from within, but more often a real person who will help you in your self-discoveries. Sometimes we do not ourselves recognize that such a guide exists for us. If the Hermit appears in a Tarot reading it may be wise to look carefully at the people around you. If you are involved in helping others find understanding then the Hermit can symbolize you in your role as guide and teacher.

When we reverse the card we corrupt the idea of withdrawal. In the same way that the High Priestess reversed can mean a fear of life, the Hermit reversed can indicate a fear of other people. If we withdraw from society as a retreat then the fact of withdrawal becomes more and more dominant, leading to phobias and paranoia. As with other trumps the negative and positive aspects of the Hermit depend on the context. The Hermit reversed can sometimes simply mean that at this moment the person needs to become involved with other people.

Because the card, when the right way up, suggests maturity the Hermit reversed can sometimes indicate a Peter Pan attitude to life. The person hangs on to basically meaningless activities, or else imitates childlike enthusiasm (like the imitation of spontaneity) as a way of avoiding the responsibilities of doing something with his or her life. I first encountered this interpretation for the Hermit reversed in a reading given by a man in New York to a friend of mine; I have since found it useful in many situations. Interestingly, I met the man through another friend who looked on the reader as a personal guide in her spiritual development.

(a) (b)   *Figure 11*   *(c)*

The Wheel of Fortune

Like certain other trump cards (most notably Death) the Wheel of
Fortune derives from a medieval homily. The Church considered
pride the greatest of sins, for in pride you set yourself before Christ.

One lesson against pride was the idea of a great king falling from power. In many versions of the King Arthur legend, the king dreams or sees before him on the eve of his final battle, a vision of a rich and powerful king seated on top of a wheel. All of a sudden the goddess Fortuna turns the wheel and the king gets crushed at the bottom. Sobered, Arthur realises that no matter how much secular power we accrue, our fate rests always in God's hands. The Visconti cards, on the right, above, enshrines this practical sermon.

Now, we might consider this neat moral fable to be far removed from the powerful and mysterious symbols staring at us from the Waite-Smith card, on the top left, and the Oswald Wirth version on the bottom left. But Fortuna and her shining hoop have a curious history. First of all, the medieval image derives from a much earlier time, when Fortuna represented the Great Goddess, and the crushed king was a real event. Every year, at mid-winter, the priestesses sacrificed the king; by imitating the death of the year they humbled themselves to the Goddess's power, and by choosing a new king they subtly suggested to her that she might once more create spring out of winter – an event by no means automatic to people who did not believe in 'natural laws' such as gravity. Thus, the Wheel originally symbolized both the mystery of nature and the human ability to take part in that mystery through a ritual sacrifice. Notice that the card comes directly below the Empress, the emblem of the Great Mother herself.

By the Middle Ages the Wheel had lost its original meaning; this did not mean that it had lost its power to suggest the mystery of life. In Thomas Malory's version of the King Arthur story we find the suggestion that the Wheel symbolizes the random turnings of 'luck'. Why do some people get rich and others poor? Why should a powerful king fall, and a formerly weak one rise to power? Who, or what, controls the turning wheel of life? Malory suggests that luck, seemingly meaningless ups and downs, is in reality fate; that is, the destiny God has chosen for each individual, based on reasons only God can understand. Because we cannot understand those reasons we say that the events of people's lives arise out of luck, but it all belongs to God's plan.

With the Wheel, therefore, we come to the great question of how and why anything happens at all in the universe. What makes the sun shine? Burning elements, yes, but what makes them burn? How did atomatic energy come into existence? Why should spring follow winter, after all? Why, and how, does gravity work? Going further, we find that fate is also an illusion, a dodge to cover up the fact that we, with our limited vision, cannot see the inner connection between all things. 'Oh well,' we say, 'it's fate', a meaningless statement because we cannot understand the meaning. Things do not just happen, they are made to happen. The power to shape events, to give life and form and purpose to the universe, belongs, Malory tells us, to the Holy Ghost, dwelling in the physical world as a presence within the Holy Grail (the Ace of Cups) in the same way that the Shekinah physically dwelt within the veiled sanctuary of the temple at Jerusalem.

We come then to the truth that both the random events of life and the so-called 'laws' of the physical universe are mysteries leading us to an awareness of the spirit force drawn down by the upraised arm of the Magician and manifested in the natural world of the Empress. A great many mystics and shamans have said that their visions showed them how all things connect, how everything fits together, because the spirit unites the entire universe. Possibly we would all see and understand this grand scheme of life, if it were not for the fact that we do not live long enough. Our short lives narrow our vision to such a miniscule portion of the world that life appears meaningless.

Now, this idea of the Wheel as the mystery of fate, with its hidden meaning, fits very well the modern Waite-Smith version of the card, especially when we consider it as halfway to the final trump. If we place the Rider pack Wheel beside the World we see immediately the link between them. In one we have a wheel filled with symbols; in the other we find a wreath of victory, and inside it a dancer who embodies the truth behind the symbols. Even more striking, we find the same four animals on each card in the corners, except that the mythological beings of card 10 have been transformed into something real and alive in the World. Thus, at the halfway point, we receive a vision of the inner meaning of life; at the end that vision has become real, embodied in our own being.

In India, the king also lost his life each year to the Goddess. When the patriarchal Aryans ended this practice the image of the turning wheel of the year became an even more powerful symbol of the new religion. The ever-turning Wheel of Life came to signify the laws of karma, leading you to reincarnate in one body after another. Now, karma is in a way simply another explanation for the mystery of fate. By the actions you take in one life, you build up a certain destiny for yourself in the next, so that if you commit a great many evil deeds you create in your immortal self a kind of psychic need for punishment. When the time comes for your next incarnation you inevitably choose a low caste or diseased body. (This simple psychological explanation of karma is perhaps based more on Buddhism than Hinduism.)

Again, our limited understanding prevents us from directly

experiencing the truth behind the Wheel of Fate, or karma. When Buddha attained enlightenment he remembered every moment of every one of his past lives. Indeed, the memory was the enlightenment. By gaining full knowledge he was able to perceive that all those lives were only forms created by his desires. When he ended his desires he 'got off the Wheel'. We could say that enlightenment means (or includes, at any rate) piercing through the outer events to the spirit that dwells within them, that is, finding the Holy Ghost within the Wheel of Fortune.

It is significant that King Arthur experiences the Wheel of Fortune as a vision in a dream. Because whether we see it as the halfway point of the Major Arcana, or simply one of the steps to completing the second line, the Wheel is indeed a vision given to us by the unconscious. The Hermit has turned away from the outer world. As a result the unconscious shows him a vision of life as a turning wheel filled with symbols.

The Wheel of Life does not become visible until we step away from it. When we are involved in it we see only the events immediately before and behind us; the daily concerns our egos find so important. When we withdraw we can see the whole pattern. Psychologically we can view this vision as an assessment a person makes of where his or her life has gone and where it is going. On a deeper level, the vision remains mysterious and symbolic. We can see what we have made of our particular lives, but fate remains a mystery.

The symbols on the Wheel all possess meaning; they help us to understand the truth within the visions. Nevertheless, we do not experience the full living force. The light of the unconscious remains veiled.

It is significant also that Malory connects the Wheel of Fortune to the Holy Grail. For the Grail symbols, which are also the symbols of the Minor Arcana, go back probably almost as far as the yearly regal sacrifice. When the candidate for initiation into the ancient European mysteries was given his 'vision' of the inner secrets of the cult it was most likely the four symbols of the cup, the sword, the lance, and the pentacle, that were shown to him with great mystic ceremony. And the basic tools of the ritual magic, laid on the Magician's table, are the same four symbols and also the suits of the Minor Arcana.

Though we do not see the four symbols directly on trump 10 we do see two of their many analogues. The four creatures on the corners of the card derive from the vision of Ezekiel 1:10. They appear also in Revelations 4:7. Now, over the centuries these four figures, sometimes called the 'guardians of heaven' came to symbolize the four basic elements of ancient and medieval science. From the right-hand corner anti-clockwise they are fire, water, air, and earth, and these elements belong as well to Wands, Cups, Swords, and Pentacles. Besides representing the elements the four beasts also stand for the four fixed signs of the zodiac – Leo, Scorpio, Aquarius, and Taurus. The zodiac, of course, is the Great Wheel of the visible universe. Thus both the elements and the signs signify the physical world, again seen as a mystery, and which can only be truly understood by learning the secret truths.

The other connection with the four elements comes in the four letter name of God on the Wheel's rim. Beginning at the upper right-hand corner, and again reading anti-clockwise, the letters are, Yod, Heh, Vav, Heh. Because this name appears in the Torah without vowels (the four letters are all consonants) it is unpronounceable; therefore God's 'true' name remains a secret. For at least two thousand years Jews and Christians have seen this name as magical. Mystics meditate on it (Abulafia's ecstatic third level of Qabalah was reached through working with God's name) and magicians manipulate it. For Qabalists the four letters are the very symbol of the world's mysteries. The process of the universe's creation was held to have occurred in four stages, corresponding to the four letters. And of course, the letters also connect with the four elements, the Grail symbols, and the Minor Arcana.

The Roman letters interspersed between the Hebrew are an anagram. Read clockwise from the top, they spell 'TARO'; read anti-clockwise they form 'TORA' (remember the High Priestess's scroll). We can also find the words 'ROTA', Latin for 'wheel', 'ORAT', Latin for 'speaks' and 'ATOR', an Egyptian goddess (also spelled 'Hathor'). Paul Foster Case, following MacGregor Mathers, founder of the Golden Dawn, has formed the sentence 'ROTA TARO ORAT TORA ATOR'. This translates as, 'The Wheel of Taro speaks the Law of Ator'. Case calls this the 'law of letters'; since Ator became best known in Egypt as a goddess of the dead, it is actually the 'law' of eternal life, concealed in the natural world. Though the body dies, the soul continues. Case also points out that the Hebrew number values of the letters of 'TARO' add up to 691, and that this, added to 26, the number value for the four letter name of God (called 'Tetragrammaton') makes 697. Those digits add up to 22, the number of letters in the Hebrew alphabet and of the trumps in the Major Arcana. And of course 22 returns us to 4.

The four symbols on the spokes are alchemical. From the top, read in a clockwise direction, they are Mercury, sulphur, water, and salt, and refer to the alchemical goal of line two, that is, transformation. Water is the symbol for dissolution, that is, dissolving the ego to release the true self that has become immersed in habits, fears, and defences. We will see just what this means when we consider Death and Temperance.

The idea of death and rebirth is also symbolized in the creatures adorning the Wheel. The snake represents Set, the Egyptian god of evil, and legendary bringer of death into the universe. It is he who kills Osiris, god of life. It is very likely that this legend, like the Wheel itself, originated in the practice in pre-history of killing the god-king, especially when we consider that Set was once a hero god, and that the snake was sacred to the Goddess who would have received the sacrifice. The snake follows the Wheel down; the jackal-headed man going up is Anubis, guide to the dead souls, and therefore giver of new life. Now, according to some legends Anubis is Set's son, and so we see that only death can bring new life, and when we fear death we are seeing only a partial truth. Psychologically, only the death of the outer self can release the life energy within.

The sphinx on top of the Wheel represents Horus, Osiris's son, and god of resurrection (in later centuries often replaced by Ator). Life has triumphed over death. But the sphinx, as we saw in the Chariot, also signifies the mystery of life. The Chariot controlled life with a strong ego. Now the sphinx has risen above the Wheel. If we allow the unconscious to speak we will sense some great secret to life, more important than the endless round of apparently meaningless events.

Set, the snake, was also called god of darkness. Again, to see darkness as 'evil' is an illusion, and indeed, the fear of darkness, like the fear of death, belongs to the ego. The ego loves the light just as the unconscious loves the dark. In light everything is simple and straightforward; the ego can occupy itself with the sense impressions from the outer world. When darkness comes the unconscious begins to stir. That is why children see monsters at night. One reason we make the outer self so strong is so we will not face demons every time the lights go out.

Those, however, who wish to go beyond the Chariot must face those terrors. Snakes and water, darkness and dissolution are all symbols of death, that is, death of the body and death of the ego. But life exists before and after the individual personality, which, of course, is only a bubble on the surface of our selves. Life is powerful, chaotic, surging with energy. Give way to it and Horus, the god of resurrection, will bring new life out of the chaos. The Wheel turns up as well as down.

The Wirth version of the Wheel of Fortune proclaims this idea even more strongly. The Wheel rests on a boat in water. Dissolution, chaos, emerge as the essential reality underlying the physical universe. All the forms of existence, the great variety of things and events, are simply momentary creations out of that powerful energy that fills the cosmos. In Hindu myth Shiva periodically destroys the entire universe, when the outer forms, like the ego, have grown weary and dull, by releasing the basic energy from which the universe originally emerged.

The number 10 suggests 0. The Fool is nothing and has no personality. But the Fool, like the number 0, is also everything, because he feels directly that energy of life, that sea surging beneath the boat. On the Rider pack Wheel of Fortune the centre of the Wheel bears no symbol. When we come to the still centre of existence, without ego or fear, all the outer forms vanish. We can understand this intuitively, but to really experience it we must allow ourselves to descend into that dark sea, to let the personality die, dissolve, and give way to the new life emerging out of darkness.

In divinatory readings the Wheel of Fortune signifies some change in the circumstances of a person's life. The person would likely not understand what has caused this change; there might be no direct reason that anyone can see, and in fact the person is likely not to be responsible in any normal sense of the word. A large corporation buys the company a man works for, and he becomes redundant. A love affair ends, not because the people have made any 'mistakes' in their treatment of each other, but simply because life continues. The Wheel turns.

The important thing about change is the reaction. Do we accept the new situation and adapt to it? Do we use it as an opportunity and find some meaning and value in it? If the Wheel appears the right way up it signifies adaptation. In its strongest sense it can indicate the ability to pierce through the mystery of events to find a greater understanding of life. The end of a love affair, despite its pain, can give greater self-knowledge.

Reversed, the card signifies a struggle against events, usually doomed because the change has happened and life will always win against the personality that tries to oppose it. If the person concerned, however, has always reacted passively to whatever life has done to him or her, then the Wheel reversed can signify a more important change than simply a new set of circumstances. It can open the way to a new awareness of responsibility for your own life.

Figure 12

Justice

The image of this trump derives from the Greek Titaness Themis, who appears, with her blindfold and scales, on court house frescoes throughout the Western world. The legal Justitia, to give her her Latin name, was blindfolded to demonstrate that the law does not discriminate and applies to weak and powerful alike. The principle of *social* justice, however, properly belongs to the Emperor, directly above Justice. Card 11 indicates that the psychic laws of Justice, by which we advance according to our ability to understand the past, depends on seeing the truth about ourselves and about life. The Tarot Justitia, therefore, wears no blindfold.

So far, we have spoken of the second line as a process of withdrawal from outer concerns to awaken the inner vision of ourselves and of life. But a vision of the underlying nature of things is meaningless if it does not produce an active response. We must always act (the Magician principle) on the wisdom received from the inner self (the High Priestess principle). Not just the perfectly balanced scales but all the images on the card point to an equilibrium between understanding and action. The figure, a woman, appears androgynous; though she sits firmly on her stone bench she looks poised to stand; one foot points outward from her robe, the other remains hidden. The sword, an emblem of action, points straight upward, indicating both resolve and the idea that wisdom is like a sword piercing through the illusion of events to find the inner meaning. Two-edged, the sword signifies choice. Life requires us to make decisions; at the same time each decision, once made, cannot be revoked. It becomes part of us. We are formed by the actions we have taken in the past; we form our future selves by the actions we take now.

The scales also represent the perfect balance of past and future. Past and future balanced, not in time, but in the clear sight of Justice staring out at you from the exact centre of the Major Arcana.

Throughout the first half of the Major Arcana, when a person involves himself in the outer world, he suffers from the illusion that he is living life on the active principle. This is because we confuse doing things with action. As we turn inwards we assume we turn away from action; and indeed the process of line two cannot be accomplished without a pause in our outer lives, or at least a shift in attention. But real action, as opposed to pointless movement, always brings meaning and value to our lives; such action comes out of understanding. Otherwise, we remain ruly passive, machines being pushed from one event to the next with no understanding of what causes us to do the things we do. The true purpose of line two is not to abandon the active principle but to awaken it.

The imagery of trump 11 combines the Magician and the High Priestess more completely than ever before. First of all, the digits of number 11 add up to 2, but the number also signifies a higher version of 1 (as well as a lesser version of 21). The woman seated before two pillars with a veil between them suggests the High Priestess, but her red robe, and her posture, one arm up, one arm down, implies the Magician. True action arises from self-knowledge; wisdom arises out of action. In life, as in the picture, the Magician and the High Priestess are inextricably combined, like a male and female snake twined around each other (symbol of the kundalini as well as the caduceus of Hermes), or the double helix of DNA. The colour of the veil is purple, emblem of inner wisdom; background, crown, hair, and scales are all yellow, signifying mental force. Wisdom does not arise spontaneously. We must think about our lives if we wish to understand them. But all our thinking goes nowhere unless it develops out of a clear vision of the truth.

On the microcosmic level of personal psychology the Wheel of Fortune represented a vision of a person's life; the events, who you are, what you've made of yourself. Justice indicates an understanding of that vision. The way to understanding lies in responsibility. As long as we believe that our past lives just happen, that we do not bring our own selves into existence through every thing we do, then the past remains a mystery, and the future an endlessly turning wheel, empty of meaning. But when we accept that every event in our lives has helped to form our characters, and that in the future we will continue to create ourselves through our actions, then the sword of wisdom cuts through the mystery.

Further, by accepting responsibility for ourselves we paradoxically free ourselves from the past. Like Buddha remembering all his lives, we can only get loose from the past by becoming conscious of it. Otherwise we constantly repeat past behaviour. This is why Justice belongs in the centre of our lives. The ego may be only a persona, a kind of mask, but that mask can control us as long as we will not admit having forged it ourselves.

The idea of responsibility for your own life does not imply any sort of invisible control over the outer world. It does not mean, for instance, that if an earthquake destroys your house you have somehow willed this to happen, for whatever hidden reasons of your own. Understanding includes accepting the limitations of your physical existence. The universe is vast and strange, and no individual can control what happens in it.

Nor does responsibility imply anything moral. It simply means that, like it or not, whatever you do, whatever you experience, contributes to the development of your personality. Life demands that you respond to every event. Not a moral requirement, just a fact of existence.

And yet all our instincts, psychology, and religion, as well as the testimony of mystics, tells us that life contains something more, an inner core independent of that outer self thrown from one experience to another. The second line shows the outer personality dying and the inner core, the angel of Temperance, being allowed to emerge. Before such a release can happen we must accept the 'justice' of our lives; what we are we have made ourselves.

Our age sees this process of awareness as primarily psychological, best exemplified in the difficult process of psychoanalysis. Other ages have externalized the process of transformation in the dramatic rituals of initiation. All initiations follow the same pattern. Having gathered his or her courage to become a neophyte the candidate first receives instruction in the teaching of the cult or mystery; during this time steps are taken, through meditation, ritual and drugs, to open the channels to the unconscious and make the person receptive. These first stages are symbolized in Strength and the Hermit. Then, in a great atmosphere of mystery and drama, the candidate is shown a vision of the cult's secret mysteries. (They are kept secret partly to protect them from unbelievers, but even more to make them effective when revealed.) In the Grail cults this vision was a dramatic procession of the Grail and its attendant symbols, carried by women weeping for a wounded king. We see an analogue of this vision in the Wheel of Fortune.

And now comes the crucial moment. The candidate must make a response. If he or she simply stands there passively waiting for the next events, then the initiation cannot continue. In the Grail cults the necessary response was most likely a question, either 'What is the meaning of these things?' or more subtly, 'Whom does the Grail serve?' By asking this question the candidate gives the cult a chance to answer, that is, to continue the initiation through the ritual death and rebirth. More important, he or she shows a recognition of being part of the process, responsible for its proper outcome. This is more difficult than it sounds. The ritual symbolizes the life, death, and rebirth of nature, as well as the body dying to release the eternal soul. To speak at such an awesome event (and remember that the initiate believed in his or her gods and goddesses in a way impossible for most of us today) required a courage at least as great as that needed to accept the truths revealed through psychological analysis and awakening.

In our time the emphasis on individualism leads us to think only of personal death and rebirth. The great iniations, on the other hand, served not only to transform the particular person, but also linked him or her to the wider mysteries of the universe. Following this lead we can see another reason why Justice belongs in the centre of the Major Arcana. We have spoken of the world as a great inter-play of opposites, a constantly turning wheel of light and dark, life and death. We have also said that at the centre of the wheel is the stationary point around which the opposites endlessly revolve. The balanced scales of Justice again suggest that stationary point. When we find the centre of our lives everything comes into balance. When all the opposites, including past and future, come into balance we are able to be free within ourselves.

Many people wonder what the Tarot, or the I Ching, or astrology tell us about free will. If the cards can predict what we will do, does that mean free will does not really exist? The question arises from a misunderstanding of free will itself; we think of it as something simple and independent of the past. At any moment, we think, we are free to do whatever we want. But our supposedly free choices are governed by our past actions. If we do not understand ourselves how can we expect to make a free choice? Only by seeing and accepting the past can we free ourselves from it.

A person may ask the cards about some situation. The cards very directly outline the consequences of some decision, say, whether or not to go ahead with a love affair, or to start some new project. Le us say that the cards indicate disaster, and that the person really can see the likelihood of what the cards predict. Now the person might say, 'Well, this is likely, but my free will allows me to change the situation'. So he or she goes ahead and the situation turns out exactly as the cards predicted. The person has not really used free will at all; rather, the idea of free will has served as an excuse for ignoring what he or she recognized as a valid projection. This is not a hypothetical situation; it happens again and again with Tarot readings. It is not enough just to foresee a likely outcome for us to change or prevent that event. We must understand why it is coming, and we must work on the causes within ourselves for the things we do and the ways we react. Free will certainly exists. We just do not know how to use it. The most important thing we can learn from Tarot readings is just how little we exercise our freedom.

In Tarot readings one should always pay very careful attention to the card of Justice. Its appearance indicates first of all that events have worked out in the way they were 'meant' to work out; that is, what is happening to you comes from situations and decisions in the past. You have what you deserve. Secondly it indicates a need and a possibility for seeing the truth of this outcome. The card signifies absolute honesty. At the same time it shows the possibility that your actions in the future can be changed by a lesson learned in the present situation.

We cannot become honest with ourselves without extending that honesty to our dealings with other people. In this sense the card carries the obvious meanings of Justice; honesty, fairness, correct actions, and of course, in legal and other matters, a just decision – though not necessarily the decision a person might prefer.

Reversed, the card indicates dishonesty with yourself and others. It shows an unwillingness to see the meaning of events and shows especially that you are missing some opportunity for a greater understanding of yourself and your life. On the outer level it indicates dishonesty and unfair actions or decisions. Sometimes it is others who are unfair to us. The reversed meaning can refer also to unjust legal decisions or to bad treatment from someone.

On the other hand we must not allow the suggestion of unfairness to act as an excuse for denying our own responsibility for what happens to us. Justice reversed sometimes reflects the attitude, 'It is unfair. Look how everybody treats me'. And on and on. Whether the right way up or reversed the clear eyes of Justice send us an overwhelming message. In the words of Emerson, 'Nothing can save you but yourself'.

(a)   *Figure 13*   (b)

The Hanged Man

After the crisis of seeing what you have made of your life comes the peace of acceptance; after Justice, the Hanged Man. Artists, writers, and psychologists have all felt drawn to this card, with its hints of great truths in a simple design. We have already referred to the occult tradition behind the upside down posture and crossed legs. In discussing Strength we said that occultists seek to release the energy of the desires and transform it into spiritual energy. Many occultists particularly the alchemists, have believed that one very direct way to do this is literally to stand on your head, so that gravity will pull down the energy from the genitals to the brain. Of course, only the most naive and optimistic alchemist would have expected such a thing to literally happen. They may have believed that trace elements found in genital fluid will seep down and affect the brain; more to the point, the reversal of physical posture serves as a very direct symbol of the reversal of attitude and experience that comes through spiritual awakening. Where everyone else is frenzied, you will know peace. Where other people believe themselves to be free, but are actually pushed from one thing to another by forces they do not understand, you will achieve true freedom by understanding and embracing those forces.

The Hanged Man hangs on a tree shaped like the letter T. Now, this is the bottom half of an ankh, Egyptian symbol of life and is sometimes called a Tau cross. According to Case the ankh in Egypt stood for the Hebrew letter Tau, which is the letter belonging to the World. Thus, the Hanged Man lies halfway to the World. We see this as well in the fact that 12 is 21 backwards, and if you turn the Hanged Man upside down (making the man himself right side up) you will have almost the same figure as the World Dancer. When we ask, therefore, what card serves as the halfway point for the Major Arcana, the answer is not one but three – the Wheel, Justice, and the Hanged Man, symbolizing a process rather than a moment.

Notice that while the Dancer extends her arms with their magic wands the Hanged Man keeps his arms crossed behind his back. Remember also that he *is* upside down. At this stage a deep spiritual awareness can only be maintained by withdrawing from society. In the World we see that same awareness maintained amidst all the outer activities of life.

He hangs on an ankh, which makes his tree the Tree of Life. Recalling Odin sacrificing himself on Yggdrasil we can also call the gallows the World Tree. This tree begins in the underworld (the unconscious), and reaches up through the physical world (the conscious) to heaven (the super-conscious). The ideas first represented by the diagram of the Lovers have begun to actually happen. What we saw previously as concepts now becomes, after Justice, a genuine experience. The Hanged Man's number, 12, is 2 times 6, that is, the High Priestess raising the Lovers to a higher level.

Beyond all its symbolism the Hanged Man affects us because it shows a direct image of peace and understanding. The calm shows so strongly in the card because the Hanged Man has surrendered to the rhythms of life. In the old initiations surrender involved joining the rituals instead of just watching them. For many modern people it involves releasing the emotions they have locked up for years. Notice that both these things are acts; surrender to the World Tree is an actual step we take, not a passive waiting.

T.S. Eliot's poem *The Wasteland* links the idea of an individual surrender to emotions with both the barrenness of European life after World War I and the ancient Grail mysteries. The wounded Fisher King can be healed by a 'moment's surrender which an age of prudence can never retract'. Earlier in the poem the hero is told 'Fear death by drowning'. The ego sees surrender as death – dissolution in the sea of life. The person who gives this warning is a Tarot reader. Eliot's poem helped to popularize Tarot cards in the 1920s. Specifically, it made famous the Hanged Man. Actually, the Hanged Man does not appear in the poem but is important because of his absence.

Eliot claimed to really know nothing of the Tarot, but only to use some images from it. Apparently, however, he knew at least one esoteric fact unknown to even many Tarot commentators – that, according to some esoteric writers the Hanged Man 'originally' bore the title, 'The Drowned Phoenician Sailor'. Madame Sosostris applies this title to the hero. 'This is your card.' Surrender is his destiny, but he has denied it: 'I do not find the Hanged Man.'

The crossed legs represent the number 4 upside down. 4 symbolizes the earth with its four directions. By reversing his own sense of values the Hanged Man has turned the world on its head. The arms and head together form a downward pointing water triangle. The way to the super-conscious is through the unconscious. The Golden Dawn card on the right of the Rider version shows the Hanged Man suspended over water. Most Tarot Qabalists assign the letter 'Mem' to this card. Mem stands for 'seas' or the element of water.

We therefore see 4, the world, consciousness, and 3, here representing water, or the unconscious, in the Hanged Man's body. These numbers multiplied form 12. In multiplication the original numbers become dissolved and form something greater than their sum.

The number 12, like 21, suggests both 1 and 2. The card reflects the Magician in the sense that the power drawn down by the wand has now entered the Hanged Man; we see it as the circle of light about his head. The experience of really feeling the spirit force within life is one of great power and excitement in the midst of complete calm. The number 2 suggests the High Priestess; so does the image of water. Both cards indicate a withdrawal, but where trump 2 indicated the archetype of receptivity, trump 12 shows an experience of it.

1 plus 2 equals 3. The Empress directly felt life through emotional involvement, the Hanged Man feels it through inner awareness.

In readings the Hanged Man bears the message of independence. Like the Fool, which signified doing what you sensed was best, even if other people thought it foolish, the Hanged Man indicates being who you are, even if others think you have everything backwards. It symbolizes the feeling of being deeply connected to life and can mean a peace that comes after some difficult trial.

The trump reversed indicates an inability to get free of social pressure. Rather than listen to our inner selves we do what others expect or demand of us. Our awareness of life always remains second-hand, never a direct experience but only a series of stereotypes, like the person who models his or her behaviour on the orders of parents and the actions of movie stars.

The card reversed also means fighting your inner self in some way. It can mean the person who tries to deny some basic part of himself or simply the person who cannot accept reality and who in some way or other is constantly battling life. By putting his or her ego against the world this person too never fully experiences life. None of us can know the full meaning of being alive until, like Odin, we hang ourselves on the World Tree, its roots deep beyond knowledge in the sea of experience, its branches lost among the endless stars.

(a) *Figure 14* (b)

Death

As much as the Lovers (directly above Death) Arthur Waite's design for trump 13 departs from standard Tarot imagery. The picture on the right, above, comes from the esoteric Golden Dawn Tarot, but, even so, illustrates the older, essentially social message of Death. Death strikes everyone, kings and commoners alike. This basic democracy of death was a favourite theme of medieval sermons. As an idea it goes back at least as far as the Jewish practice of burying everyone in the same style, a white shroud and a plain pine box, so that in death rich become level with the poor.

As we might guess, the great power of death leads us beyond democracy to both philosophical and psychological meanings. Death, like life, is eternal and always present. Individual forms are always dying while others come into existence. Without death to clear away the old, nothing new could find a place in the world. Many science fiction novels have shown the tyrannical society that would result if the world's leaders did not die. The liberation of Spain after the death of Franco aptly demonstrated death's importance.

When we die our flesh decays, leaving only the skeleton. That too will eventually pass but it lasts long enough to at least hint at eternity. Therefore, the skeleton in the Golden Dawn card implies that eternity triumphs over the transitory. Now, the skeleton has an occult meaning as well. All over the world the training for shamans includes methods of seeing one's own skeleton, using drugs, meditation, even scraping the skin off the face. By freeing the bone from the flesh shamans connect themselves to eternity.

Because people fear death they seek reason and value in it. The Christian religion teaches us that death liberates our souls from the sinful flesh so that we may join God in a greater life to come. Carl Jung has written of the value of believing in an afterlife. Without it, death may seem too monstrous to accept.

Other people have pointed out that death joins us to nature. The consciousness that isolates us from the world will be obliterated; though the body will decay, that only means that it is feeding other creatures. Each death brings new life. Many people find the notion of themselves being eaten horrible to contemplate. The modern practice of embalming and painting corpses so that they look alive, and then of burying them in sealed metal caskets derives from the desire to maintain the body's separateness from nature even in death.

The fact is, since we will not know what happens to our bodies once the spirit has left them, what we really fear is the destruction of the personality. It is the ego that sees itself as separate from life; because it is only a mask the ego does not wish to die. It wishes to make itself superior to the universe.

If we can accept death we will be able to live more fully. The ego never wants to release energy; it tries to hoard it against the fear of death. As a result new energy cannot get in. We see this very graphically in people's breathing when they panic. They try to gulp air in without letting any out and as a result become short of breath.

In sex too the ego hoards energy. It fights climax and surrender because at that moment the ego partly dissolves. In Elizabethan England sexual intercourse was often called 'dying'. And Death in the Tarot comes below the Lovers.

Because the ego resists the very idea of death and therefore keeps us from enjoying life we must sometimes take extreme steps to get past it. The initiation rites always led up to a simulated death and rebirth. The initiate is led to believe that he or she is actually about to die. Everything is done to make this death as real as possible so that the ego will be tricked and in fact experience that dreaded dissolution. Then, when the initiate is 'reborn' he or she experiences a new maturity and a new freedom of energy. In recent years many people have experienced something very like these rites through using psychedelic drugs. They believe they are dying and they feel themselves reborn. However, without the preparation symbolized in the Hanged Man the experience can often be deeply disturbing.

Contrary to what many people believe the card of Death does not actually refer to transformation. Rather, it shows us the precise moment at which we give up the old masks and allow the transformation to take place. Perhaps we can understand this better if we consider the Tarot's parallel in psychotherapy. By force of will (Strength) the person, with the help of the therapist-guide (the Hermit), allows knowledge to emerge of who he or she really is, and what habits or fears he or she wishes to shed (Wheel and Justice). This knowledge brings calm and a desire to change (the Hanged Man). But then a fear sets in. 'If I give up my behaviour', the person thinks, 'maybe there will be nothing left. I will die.' We live under the ego's control for so many years we come to believe that nothing else exists. The mask is all we know. Often people will stay stuck in therapy for years because they fear release. The nothingness of the Fool terrifies them.

People who have been fat for years often experience a similar fear if they try to diet. 'I have always been fat', they think. 'I am a fat person. If I get skinny I will not exist any more.' The fact is, this is true. The 'I' that was a fat person will no longer exist. But something else will emerge.

The Waite image for trump 13 increases the psychological meaning of the card. The four people demonstrate different approaches to change. The king, struck down, shows the rigid ego. If life comes at us with enough power the ego may collapse; insanity can result from an inability to adjust to extreme change. The priest stands and faces Death directly; he can do so because his stiff robes and hat protect him and support him. We see here the value of a code of belief to help us past our fears of death. The Maiden symbolizes partial innocence. The ego is not rigid, yet still aware of itself, unwilling to surrender. Therefore she kneels but turns away. Only the child, representing complete innocence, faces Death with a simple offering of flowers.

Death wears black armour. We have already seen how blackness and darkness symbolize the source of life as well as its end. Black absorbs all colour; death absorbs all individual lives. The skeleton rides a white horse. White repels all colours and therefore symbolizes purity, but also nothingness. The white rose stands for the desires purified, for when the ego dies selfish and repressive needs die with it.

At the back of the card we see a sun rising between two pillars. The ego belongs to the outer world of duality, separating and categorizing experience. Through Death we feel the radiant power of Life, which knows only itself. The landscape before the pillars reminds us of the 'land of the Dead' described in all mythologies. We fear the death of our old selves because we do not know what to expect afterwards. One main function of those shamans who see their skeletons is to go ahead through the Land of the Dead and thus be able to guide the souls of others.

A river flows through the middle of the card. Rivers, as we saw with the Empress, indicate the unity of change and eternity. The fact that they lead to the sea reminds us of the formlessness and oneness of the universe. The boat, reminiscent of the Pharaohs' burial boats, symbolizes the true self carried through Death to a new life.

No matter the picture, all Tarot cards bear the number 13. Though most people consider 13 unlucky they do not know why. In our culture 13 refers to Judas, since he was the thirteenth man at the Last Supper, and therefore the number indicates Christ's (and all people's) death. Friday the thirteenth is especially unlucky because Christ died on a Friday. But we can also describe Christ as the thirteenth man. Death leads to resurrection.

In a more symbolic sense 13 is unlucky because it takes us beyond 12. 12 is something of a 'perfect' number. It combines the archetypes of 1 and 2, it symbolizes the zodiac and therefore the universe, it can be divided by 1, 2, 3, 4, and 6, more digits than any other number. 13 destroys this elegance. It can be divided by nothing but 1 and itself. Again, we can go beyond the negative aspects of the symbolism. Precisely because it ruins the perfection of 12, 13 signifies a new creation; death breaks up old forms and makes way for the new.

The number 13 adds up to 4, the Emperor. Through Death we overcome our outer 'social' selves. Since 13 is a higher form of 3 the card also recalls the Empress, and reminds us again that in nature life and death are inseparable.

In divinatory readings Death signifies a time of change. Often, it indicates a fear of change. In its most positive aspect it shows a clearing away of old habits and rigidness to allow a new life to emerge. In its most negative aspect it indicates a crippling fear of physical death. This fear goes deeper than many people realize, and often a reading with many positive indications will end badly because of Death in the position of fears.

The trump reversed indicates being stuck in old habits. Waite talks of, 'inertia, sleep, lethargy' in life. This sense of a sluggish, boring life masks the sometimes desperate battle of the ego to avoid change. The card always indicates that Death, with its subsequent rebirth, is not only a possibility but also, in a sense, a necessity. The moment has come to die. By drowning us in lethargy, the ego prevents awareness of this fact from coming to consciousness. Inertia, boredom and depression often conceal inner terrors.

Temperance

The Chariot symbolized the successful construction of an ego able to deal victoriously with life. As time goes by this ego becomes rigid; slowly behaviour becomes less a response to reality and more and more a string of habits. The purpose of the second line of the Major Arcana is to free us from this artificial personality, and at the same time give us a glimpse of the greater truths within the universe. Temperance, appearing below the Chariot, shows a person whose behaviour is once again connected to the real world but in a way more meaningful than ever before. For if the child relates directly to life it does so without consciousness, and as consciousness grows so does the ego. Temperance indicates the ability to combine spontaneity with knowledge.

The term 'temperance' means moderation. For most people this means self control. The Tarot Temperance, however, does not go to extremes simply because extremes are not necessary. Not an artificial inhibition according to a moral code, but exactly the opposite; a true and proper response to all situations as they arise.

The word 'temperance' derives from the Latin 'temperare' which means 'to mix' or 'to combine properly'. The person who has released his or her inner self is characterized not only by moderation but by an ability to combine the different sides of life. Many people can only deal with life by parcelling it off into sections. They create one personality for business and another for their private lives; both are false. They consider certain moments and situations to be 'serious' and others to be 'fun' and are careful never to smile at a serious subject. The people they love are often not the people whom they find sexually attractive. All these separations derive from the inability to take life as it comes, moment by moment. Temperance combines the elements of life. In reality it combines the elements of the personality, so that the person and the outer world will flow together naturally.

(a)   *(b)*   *(c)*
Figure 15

The trump displays the signs of combination all through the picture. When we look at the Waite-Smith image on the left we see first of all the water being poured from one cup to another; the elements of life flowing together. Notice that the lower cup is not directly below the upper, so that the picture shows a physical impossibility. To other people the Temperate person's ability to handle all life's problems with joy appears magical.

The Rider pact Temperance presents both cups as magical. In the Wirth picture on the right the upper one is silver, indicating a flow from the Moon, that is, the unconscious, to the Sun, consciousness. The second line began with a withdrawal from the world to find the inner self; the time has now come to return to the normal activities of life.

The road especially signifies return. We have gone down into the self and now we are making our way back to involvement with the outer world, enriched. Notice that the two pillars of the earlier cards have become two mountains. Abstract ideas are becoming reality; Temperance is a card of behaviour, not concepts.

The angel stands with one foot on land, one foot in water. As the water represents the unconscious so the land symbolizes the 'real world' of events and the other people. The Temperate personality, acting from an inner sense of life, links the two realms. The water also indicates potentiality, that is, the possibilities of life, while the land symbolizes manifestation or actuality. The Temperate person, through his or her actions, brings into reality the wonders sensed by the Hanged Man.

The BOTA Temperance (see fig. 15b) shows water being poured on a lion, and a torch dripping flames on an eagle. Leo symbolizes fire (the Magician), while the eagle, the 'higher' form of Scorpio, stands for water (the High Priestess). The angel is mixing the basic duality, inseparably combining the different sides of life that previously appeared hopelessly alien to each other. Now, the eagle stands for the higher Scorpio because Scorpio represents the energy of the unconscious. As the lower form, the scorpion, this energy shows itself primarily as sexuality, the 'animal desires' of the undeveloped personality. When the energy has been transformed by channelling it through awareness it becomes the eagle of spirituality. Strength showed this energy brought out in the form of the lion; in the BOTA Temperance we see the process completed, the eagle and the lion combined.

The angel resembles the Greek goddess Iris, whose sign was the rainbow; a rainbow appears on the BOTA card and iris flowers on the Rider pack version. Rainbows appear as a sign of peace after a storm, which reminds us that Temperance shows the personality released by the fearful experience of Death. The rainbow comes from water yet shines as light across the sky, an emblem of the inner self, which once seemed dark, chaotic, fearful, brought out and joyously transformed into the promise of new life. In Jewish and Christian tradition the rainbow is a sign of renewal after the Flood. The Flood, like Shiva's destruction of the universe, stands psychologically for the death of old patterns, which do not reflect the truth and joy of life and which lead people into 'evil' – behaviour destructive to themselves and to others.

As Zeus's messenger Iris travelled to the underworld to fill her golden cup with water from the River Styx. The Greeks believed that dead souls travelled across the Styx to the land of the dead. Only a descent into the underworld of the self can renew life.

Religiously the angel symbolizes the immortal soul liberated by death. If you look closely below the collar you will see God's name worked into the fabric of the gown. In Christian tradition the soul will become joined with God after the resurrection. The triangle within the square indicates that the Spirit rises from within the material body.

Psychologically the angel indicates the energy of life which emerges after the ego's Death. The triangle now shows that this energy works within the square of ordinary activities. We do not need to perform miracles to sense our connection with the immortal universe. We need only be ourselves.

Remember that the Tetragrammaton appeared on the Wheel as a mystery of fate. Here the name has become part of us. We become 'masters' of our fate when we learn to deal with life as it comes and not according to routines of habits and defences.

The divinatory meanings, like the card's ideas, begin with moderation, balance in all things and taking the middle path. The card means right action, doing the correct thing in whatever situation arises. Very often this means doing nothing. The intemperate person always needs to be doing something, but very often a situation requires a person to simply wait. The card will sometimes appear as an antidote to cards of recklessness and hysteria.

Temperance signifies mixing disparate elements together, blending activities and feelings to produce a sense of harmony and peace. Because it means balancing and combining the different sides of life Temperance carries a special significance for the Minor Arcana. If a reading shows a person split between say, wands and cups, activity and passivity, or cups and pentacles, fantasy and reality, then Temperance, moderation and acting from an inner sense of life, can give a clue to bringing these things together.

Like the Fool reversed Temperance upside down indicates a wildness, going to extremes. In Temperance this is because the person lacks the inner awareness to know what is appropriate to a situation. The trump reversed can act as a warning that you have allowed your life to become fragmented and that you are sliding from one extreme to another. It can in fact indicate failure in the great task of letting old habits and fears die away into the past. On a simple level the reversed Temperance tells us to calm down and avoid extremes; in its deepest sense it sends us back to Strength to begin that long, sometimes painful, sometimes frightening, but always essentially joyous process of death and rebirth.

Chapter 6.
The Great Journey

The Goal of Enlightenment

ost people find fulfilment when they have destroyed the mask of the persona and are able to return to the ordinary world, renewed. However, there have always been people who have sought something greater – a complete union with the spiritual foundations of reality. For them it is not enough to simply sense this spirit running through their lives. They wish to know this force in full consciousness and their enlightenment, teachings and example enrich the rest of us. For these people the achievement of the second line is a preparation and a clearing away of obstacles.

In its truest form life is simply pure, undifferentiated energy in which everything living exists at once. There are no forms, no parts and pieces of eternity. Consciousness protects us from such overwhelming experience. It breaks down the totality of life into opposites and categories. In the Hanged Man and Temperance we partly reach beyond these limiting illusions to a sense of life's great power, and a sense of ourselves as part of that power. But even in Temperance the illusion of separateness returns. The card below Temperance is called the World because it is through experiencing it we and the universe become one.

The line begins with a paradox, a seeming fall into the illusions of the Devil. By pursuing the meaning of the card at this particular place we come to a new understanding of what is involved in liberation. At the beginning of the Major Arcana we said that darkness and light were bound up together. The dark unconscious side, however, lay hidden in the temple of the High Priestess, to be experienced only through intuition. To get beyond the veil we must first go into the darkness of the self. Many religions celebrated the passage through darkness to the land of eternal life. When the

Christian Church established its religion of light it banished all evocations of darkness as evil. The common image of the Devil is simply a mixture of the Greek god Pan and various other competitors of Christ.

The Tower's meaning depends on how we view the Devil. If we see the Devil as simply illusions then the Tower shows them shattered by violent upheaval. However, if the Devil signifies release of repressed energy then the illusion shattered by the lightning is nothing less than the veil of consciousness itself.

In each line the middle three cards form a special group. For the first it was the triad of nature, society, and education; for the second it was the change, through Justice, from the outer vision of the Wheel to the inner experience of the Hanged Man. In the last line the three cards show the passage from the inner revelation of the Star back to the consciousness of the Sun. In between, filled with strangeness, lies the Moon.

The Sun is not the end. Once more we descend into darkness to experience, in Judgement and the World, a total joining with the universe and the spirit that fills it. We are now able to act in the outer world while never losing that sense of vastness and wonder within. The Magician and the High Priestess united in one joyful dance.

Figure 16

The Devil

Why does this grim figure of oppression appear so late in the Tarot? After achieving the balance of Temperance why fall so abruptly? The Devil bears the number 15, which reduces to 6, the Lovers, and in fact, we can say that Waite worked backwards from the Devil when he designed his radical version of the Lovers. Thus in the Rider pack the Devil, with his captured demons, appears as a perversion of trump 6. But why the 'true' card so early and the perversion so near the end?

The Devil introduces the last line. This hints that it provides some vital energy for the work of that line. Now, the line deals with archetypal forces beyond the self. Does the road to enlightenment take us through the dark world of the Devil? Remember that Dantë goes through Hell before he can reach Purgatory and Paradise; and that William Blake, the occultist and poet, described the Devil as the true hero of Milton's moralist poem *Paradise Lost*.

In order to understand the esoteric value of the Devil we must first consider its more usual meanings as a force of illusion and oppression. The main illusion is materialism, a term which we usually think of as an over concern with money, but which more properly means the view that nothing exists beyond the world of the senses. The Devil perches on a block of stone similar to the

Emperor's cube in the BOTA deck. But where that cube symbolized the entire universe the Devil's rectangle, half a cube, indicates a incomplete knowledge.

Denying any spiritual component to life the materialist pursues only personal desires – monetary, sexual and political. Since such narrowness often leads to unhappiness the Devil has come to symbolize misery. When we look at the two figures, however, we do not observe any discomfort in their faces or posture. Notice also that the chains do not really hold them; the large loops can easily come off. The Devil's power rests in the illusion that nothing else exists. In a great many situations, from political oppression to the personal misery of a bad family life, people only become consciously unhappy when they realize that life holds other alternatives.

The Devil's posture, one hand up, one down, recalls the Magician. Where trump 1 raises a wand to heaven, bringing down spiritual power, the Devil's torch points to earth, signifying the belief that nothing exists beyond the material.

The Devil's palm bears the astrological glyph for Saturn, a planet often seen as symbolizing evil or misfortune, but more properly viewed as limitations, weaknesses or restrictions. The outspread fingers plus the number 5 in 15, recall the Hierophant's two fingers up, two down. Where the latter gesture signified that there was more to the universe than what you can see before you, the Devil's open palm indicates again that nothing exists beyond the obvious.

The Devil wears a reversed pentacle, a symbol of black magic, on his forehead. Now, the pentacle carries a great many significances. If you stand with your feet apart and your arms out you will see that the pentacle symbolizes the human body. The right way up the head is uppermost and when we reverse the pentacle the genitals are above the head. In traditional Christian teaching the power of reason, the ability to tell right from wrong, rules the desires. Therefore, the reversed pentacle indicates letting your desires overpower your judgement. The Devil's torch inflames the man's tail, and people who experience their sexual needs as both over-powering and destructive have often described it as a fire burning inside them. The card's background is black, symbolizing black magic, the inability to see the truth and depression.

Thus we see the Devil's traditional meanings: illusion, materialism, misery and sexual obsession. And yet, the card carries a great force. The Devil stares out at us intensely. Practitioners of Tantra describe the kundalini as a fire in the body, beginning at the root of the spine, the tailbone, and evoked by sexual rites.

Consider again the pentacle. The sex organs over the head. The image reminds us of the Rider pack Lovers, where the woman symbol of the unconscious and the passions, looks to the angel. We can also recall Strength, directly above the Devil, where the lion symbolizes the animal energy raised up and tamed. We have already spoken of the occult belief that sexual and spiritual energy are actually one and the same, symbolized by Scorpio's double image of scorpion and eagle. Strange as it sounds this idea is not really so mysterious. It takes neither an occultist nor a Freudian to recognize the great power of sex in our lives. How much of popular culture, with its love songs, romantic movies, and sexual jokes and slang, is devoted to it? If, for the average person, the sex urge is so dominant, then it makes sense that the occultist should seek to tap this energy and raise it to such a level that eventually it becomes wholly transformed into the overwhelming experience of enlightenment.

A more subtle point – dreaming is always accompanied by the body's sexual arousal, an erect penis or clitoris, plus other indications. Now, a dream is the unconscious manifesting itself as images. The indication is that the unconscious is sexual in nature and that dreams are a partial transformation of that energy into a wider form. In fact, the term 'unconscious' does not really refer to the dreams and myths which reveal it to us, but rather to the great pool of energy which sustains us through life.

Our Western culture has taught us that the body and the spirit are fundamentally opposed. We assume that the monk and nun abstain from sex so as not to contaminate themselves. But we can look at celibacy in another way. By refraining from sex the celibate can turn that energy in another direction. In India, the connection between sexual and spiritual energy has always been recognized. Shiva's symbol is a phallus, while the Tantra rites call for copulation as a way of charging the body with energy. The Gnostics, a major influence on European occult ideas, practised rites very similar to Tantra. And the Gnostics, like Blake after them, considered Satan the true hero of the Garden of Eden, seeking to give Adam and Eve knowledge of their true selves.

If the way to spirit leads through the desires, then why does society repress them? And if the path to liberation has been known and mapped out for centuries why keep it a secret? The answer to these questions lies in the terrible power of sexual-spiritual energy. If raised to the higher level it frees us from the limitations of duality. However, if the power is released and not transformed it can result in obsessions, sexual crimes, violence and even the destruction of the personality. It was not simply sexual politics that led the Greek patriarchs to attack the female-dominated mysteries of ecstatic rapture. Overwhelmed by the forces released within themselves, the worshippers would whip and mutilate themselves, and sometimes rage through the countryside, tearing to pieces animals, men and even children who were not safely locked indoors. It is only the person who has been trained, who has achieved a deep level of inner peace, who has, in fact, reached the understanding the Tarot calls Temperance, who can deal safely with the forces implied in the Devil.

Actually, the Devil implies a great deal more than sexual rites and violent energy. On a wider sense it symbolizes the life energy locked up in the dark hidden areas of the self, which cannot be entered by ordinary means. It is called the Devil because for those who are not prepared to receive this energy it can manifest itself as monsters, a sense of the universe as filled with evil, or the temptation to indulge in violence. We said in the second line that the child develops a strong ego so it will no longer fear the darkness. The action of the second line gave us a glimpse of the dark waters beneath the Wheel of Life. The third line requires a complete release of unconscious energy. Such a flood can only come through entering that hidden area, with all its illusions, horrors, and desires which can so easily distract the unprepared from the final goal.

Look again at the gestures of the Hierophant and the Devil. The priest's two fingers held down signify that there is more to life than what we see; at the same time the fingers imply that the path to that deeper knowledge is closed. The Devil's open fingers can symbolize the narrow illusion of thinking that what you see is all that exists; or it can symbolize seeing everything. Nothing hidden away. The specific gesture made by the Devil, with a gap between the two double fingers, is the gesture made by the High Priest in Jerusalem to bring down the spirit force. It survives today in the Jewish New Year celebration as part of the 'priestly blessing'.

Paul Douglas has called trump 15 the 'dark side of the collective unconscious'. When the so-called 'black magician' (once a title for the Devil) conjures a demon he or she is actually bringing out a force from inside the self. If the operation goes successfully the magician masters the demon, making it his or her servant. That is, the magician uses the liberated energy rather than falling a prey to it. To do this, the magician must be purified of ego desires and of fear. In short, he or she must have achieved Temperance, otherwise the demon can 'win' the encounter. The magician becomes a slave to the illusions of the Devil.

We have gone quite deeply into a radical interpretation of the Devil. The card's divinatory meanings tend to follow the more usual interpretations. We take the more obvious meanings because in a reading the card appears out of context. The Devil can indicate a narrow materialistic view of life; it can mean any form of misery or depression, especially feeling chained or imprisoned, with the illusion that no alternatives are possible. If it appears in connection with the Lovers it shows that a relationship which began with love has turned into a trap.

The Devil signifies being the slave of your desires, rather than acting the way you think is best. It can mean a controlling obsession, particularly a sexual one, where the person feels drawn to commit acts he or she finds morally repugnant. The extreme example is the sex criminal; on a much more common level many men and women find themselves powerfully attracted to people they actively dislike. The feeling of helplessness and shame which results from giving in to these desires belongs to the Devil.

Earlier we observed the calm on the faces of the chained men and women. This indicates the acceptance of a bad situation. Eventually we come to view our unhappy conditions as normal, and may even fight against change. The Devil reversed, on the other hand, indicates an attempt to break loose from some misery or bondage, either real or psychological. The person no longer accepts his or her situation and moves towards liberation. Paradoxically it is precisely at such a time that we feel our unhappiness and the limitations of our lives most strongly. Before you can slip off the chains you must become conscious of them. Therefore, people who are undergoing some process of liberation – say, leaving home, psychotherapy or a difficult divorce – often find themselves far more unhappy than when they blindly accepted their oppressed condition. Such a period can be crucial to a person's development. If one can survive it, one will emerge happier and with a more developed personality. Sometimes we can find the period of transition unbearably painful and slip back to our chains.

The Devil reversed in the position of the past often means that the change has occurred, but the feelings of sadness, of anger, of depression remain, perhaps hidden from conscious view, but still an influence. We must often deal with the devils of the past, even those we have long ago overcome in practical terms. The psyche never lets anything go; it never simply forgets about anything. The way to liberation lies in using and transforming the knowledge and energy bound up in every experience.

Figure 17

The Tower

Like the Devil, this trump carries a great many meanings, and the explanations given by most Tarot books indicate its surface moral lessons. The Tower is said to be the materialist conception of the universe, and the lightning the destruction that comes to a life based on purely materialist principles. Even here we find a great deal of subtlety. While it may appear that some outside force strikes down the narrow-minded person, the violence shown in the card actually derives from psychological principles. The person who lives only to satisfy the ego demands of wealth, fame, and physical pleasure, ignoring both introspection and the spiritual beauty of the universe, raises a prison around himself. We see this person as the Tower; grey, rock-bound, with a gold crown. At the same time a pressure builds up inside the mind as the unconscious strains at its bonds. Dreams become disturbed, arguments and depression more common, and if a person represses these manifestations as well, the unconscious will often find some way to explode.

The explosion may appear as an external disaster; your friends and family turn against you, your work collapses and violence of one kind or another swirls around you. And it is true that one of the mysteries of life is the way that bad luck comes in clusters. Yet, how many of these problems result from long neglected or mishandled situations, striking us at the moment we become vulnerable? And if some problems, illness or death of people close to us, economic problems in society, even natural disasters, such as storms – or lightning bolts – appear at the same time as personal problems, such coincidence shows again that life does indeed contain more than we can see in front of us.

We should not think that the psyche, or life, brings on disaster simply to punish us. The drops of fire falling on each side of the Tower are shaped like the Hebrew letter yod, the first letter of God's name. They symbolize not anger, but grace. The universe, and the human mind will not allow us to stay forever imprisoned in our towers of illusion and repression. If we cannot free ourselves peacefully then the forces of life will arrange an explosion.

I do not mean to imply that we in any way enjoy the painful experiences that shake us loose, or that we can see the beneficial ends from such means, or even that the process always results in freedom. Very often a series of disasters or a period of violent emotions will cripple a once strong personality. The point is only that given no other outlets the unconscious will erupt all around us, and that we can use this experience to find a better balance. Some decks call this card 'The House of the Devil'; but others call it 'The House of God', reminding us that it is spiritual force which destroys our psychic prisons.

There is a deeper meaning in the linking of God's and the Devil's houses, a meaning implied even more directly in the fact that the Hebrew for 'snake' bears the same numerical value (and is therefore seen as equivalent to) the word for 'messiah'. The Devil is God's shadow. In trump 15 we saw that the person seeking unity with life must bring out the energy normally repressed by the conscious personality. By embracing the Devil, however, we endanger that calm and balance shown in Temperance. We set the psyche on a violent course leading to the explosion of the Tower. Jung described consciousness as a dam blocking free flow of the river of the unconscious. Temperance acts as a kind of sluice, letting the waters through at a controlled rate. The Tower blows away the dam completely, releasing the locked up energy as a flood.

Why take such a dangerous course? The answer is that no other way exists to finally go beyond the barrier of consciousness, or to break free from that which separates life into opposites and which cuts us off from the pure energy contained within ourselves. The veil across the temple is the conscious personality, protecting us from life itself. As mystics, shamans, and ecstatics have testified, eternity is all around us, blinding and overwhelming. The unprepared mind cannot encompass such power, and so consciousness comes to our rescue, closing off the major part of our spiritual energy, parcelling experience into time and opposing categories.

The mystics tell us as well that revelation comes as a lightning bolt which destroys the illusions of the material world in a single blinding flash, like that seen by Paul on his way to Damascus, or that which struck Buddha under the Bo tree. No matter how long the meditation, the years of prayer or occult training, the truth comes all at once or it does not come at all. Which is not to say that the preparation was meaningless. The work shown in the first two lines of the Major Arcana serves a double purpose. Not only does it make us strong enough to withstand the lightning when it comes, it also puts us in a position to bring about the lightning. All occult practices begin with one assumption: that it is possible to call down the bolt of revelation, that a person can take definite steps to make this happen.

These steps include the teaching, the meditations, the ego death, and finally the embracing of the Devil. By releasing that energy we get past the barriers of repression and open ourselves to the lightning. For the spirit exists all the time; it is we who are blind to it. By going into the darkness of the self we open ourselves to the light.

Obviously, this is a dangerous process. The unprepared person can become trapped in the illusions of the Devil. We will see also that the release of energy carries its own dangers as the psyche tries to integrate it with the conscious awareness. The hero on the way back from the centre of the labyrinth can become lost if he has not carefully prepared himself.

The Tower comes below the High Priestess, for it shows the veil being ripped away. At the same time the lightning recalls the Magician. That energy and truth which passes through the Magician here strikes in full force. We also see trumps 1 and 2 in the two people; one in blue, the other in a red cloak. The polarity symbolized in so many of the earlier cards is here overwhelmed by the unity of existence. Count the yod drops of fire and you will find that they come to twenty-two, the number of trumps. You will find also that they are separated into ten and twelve. The Sumerians used a number system based on ten (for ten fingers) for worldly matters, but a separate system based on twelve, for the zodiac, for spiritual counting. This duality is also an illusion. Both worlds are manifestations of the same spirit fire.

The image of a destroyed tower brings to mind the tower of Babel. On a literal level that story explains why people speak so many languages, while morally it teaches us not to put our faith in human abilities (the Tower as materialism). But we can see another meaning in Babel's destruction. The lightning that struck it was God speaking directly to humanity rather than indirectly through the ordinary phenomena of the physical world.

In an instant the speech of God replaces the human speech that built the tower; revelation replaces the step by step knowledge of the senses. Remember that the descent of the spirit at Pentecost scrambles human language; people 'speak in tongues' or make animal noises. And the shamans in their trances speak the languages of the beasts and birds. Human language is an aspect of culture and a limitation of consciousness. Many linguists, notably Benjamin Whorf, have demonstrated that our languages restrict our ability to perceive reality, like a filter over the universe. And truth, the mystics tell us, cannot be expressed in words.

The Tower's 16 reduces to 7, the Chariot, linked by Case and others to human speech. The speech of God of the Tower destroys in a moment all the careful constructions of culture, language and consciousness. In so doing it returns us to the chaos of the sea beneath the Wheel of Fortune and the Pool of water behind the veil of the Priestess.

In some ways the Tower is the most complex of all the trumps; its more subtle meanings are at odds with its obvious ones. Like the Devil its divinatory meanings usually derive from the obvious. It usually refers to a period of violent upheaval (either literally or psychologically), the destruction of long established situations, the break-up of relationships in anger or even violence.

Because the card carries such furious significance many people recoil at the sight of it. The reaction raises the vital question of how to regard the Tarot's more fearful images. We must learn to use all experience, the Tower as well as the Lovers. When the Tower appears it is necessary to remember that it can lead to freedom; the explosions are clearing away some situation that has built up intolerable pressure. They can lead to new beginnings.

To say that the Tower's appearance usually signifies difficult experience is not to insist that the deeper meanings will never arise. The card can mean a flash of enlightenment, particularly if such enlightenment replaces a limited view of life. Only the reader's intuition and experience, as well as the hints from the other cards, can indicate the specific meaning.

The Tower reversed indicates a modified version of the card's meaning when the right way up. The violence and storm are still there but milder. At the same time the reversed trump carries the extra meaning of 'imprisonment', to use Waite's term. This paradox becomes resolved when we consider that when the right way up the Tower liberates. When reversed, then, the card means that we do not allow ourselves to undergo the full experience. By keeping a tight control on our reactions we lessen the pain; we also do not release all the repressed material. Within ourselves the painful experience continues, never having gone its full course. By shielding the Tower from the lightning we become its prisoners.

Figure 18

The Star

After the storm, peace. The person who undergoes emotional upheaval finds afterward a sense of calm and emptiness. Lay the cards out for someone who has never seen them and the Star will hardly need interpretation. Everything in it speaks of wholeness, openness, and healing.

It is worth comparing the Star with Temperance, where we also see a figure pouring water and holding two cups, with one foot on land and one in water. Both cards come after a crisis, but where Temperance is controlled the Star is free. Not clothed, but naked. Not standing stiffly, but supple and relaxed. And finally, where Temperance pours the water back and forth, blending but at the same time conserving, the Star maiden pours it out freely, confident that life will continually supply her with new energy. The picture suggests all those mythical chalices that could never be emptied.

The Tower's release of energy ripped away the veil of

consciousness. Here in the Star we are behind the veil. The pool of water, small though it is, represents the unconscious; that same water we saw concealed behind the pillars of the High Priestess. Now this universal life energy has been stirred up by the act of pouring the person's own life waters into it.

The water being poured onto land indicates that the energy freed by the Tower is directed outwards as well as inwards; it links the unconscious with the outer reality of the physical world. One way to describe the streams of water is as the archetypes of myth, the images through which the unconscious expresses itself. The unconscious is a whole, without shape or division, but it emerges into awareness through the separate streams of mythology. With the Star we have gone beyond myth to its source as formless energy; as light coming out of darkness. The transformation of darkness into light is the unconscious, the hidden vastness within us, changed into the ecstatic awareness of super-consciousness.

One stream of water flows back into the pool, signifying that all archetypes blend back into the formless truth. The value of the archetype lies only in its power to arouse the inner self and to connect us to the source. The maiden's foot does not penetrate the water. The collective unconscious has not been entered, but only stirred up.

The bird on the right is an ibis, a symbol of the Egyptian god Thoth, who was considered the inventor of all arts, from poetry to pottery. Literally he taught the first artists their techniques, but on a more symbolic level, we can say that all creative action stems originally from the pool of unformed energy. It is one function of being a physical creature that we take this energy and use it to make poems, paintings and tapestries. All these human creations are symbolized in those several streams of water. Every act of creation objectifies spiritual energy in the thing created. At the same time no work exhausts the artist's inspiration as long as he or she remains connected to the inner sources. Therefore, the one stream returns to the pool, just as each work gives its creator new inspiration.

The Star appears below the Empress and the Wheel. In the Empress we saw the natural world glorified in the passions. But the Empress was heavily clothed to indicate that she expresses her emotion through things outside herself – nature, lovers and children. In the Star we see the inner self joyfully experiencing itself. The Star maiden combines the two female archetypes, the inner sensitivity of the High Priestess brought out and expressed with the passion of the Empress.

In the Wheel of Fortune we saw a vision of the universe in

mysterious symbols. Here the Tower has taken us beyond visions. In the Star we directly experience the unconscious, rather than its images.

As trump 17 the Star goes beyond 7, with the Star releasing the life force that the Chariot controlled and directed. 1 plus 7 equals 8, and we can see that the Star is Strength raised to a higher level, with the lion of desire no longer simply tamed, but transformed into light and joy.

The stars on the card are all eight pointed which is another reference to Strength. Since an eight pointed star can be formed by placing one square over another with the points alternating, the octogram is sometimes thought of as halfway between the square and the circle. The square stands for matter and the circle for spirit. Human beings are the link between the spirit and the physical world; our ability to both feel the truth, and to act, makes us vehicles through which the truth can manifest itself.

The Church used to describe humans as halfway between the animals and the angels. Usually a moral interpretation was given; people could follow their desires or their reason. But we can use this metaphor to say that human awareness and action connect the physical world to the 'angels'.

Despite all the suggestions of manifestations the Star is not really a card of action, but of inner calm. In contrast to Temperance and the Moon, the Star shows no road leading back from the pool to the mountains of outer reality. Though the streams and the ibis imply the uses of creative energy, the experience of the Star is one of peace. For the moment, the journey can wait.

In divinatory readings the card expresses hope, a sense of healing and wholeness, especially after emotional storms. Very often the Star and the Tower suggest each other even when only one actually appears. Trump 17 indicates the unconscious activated, but in a very benign way.

Reversed, we close ourselves off from the card's calm and hope, experiencing weakness, impotence, and fear. This deep insecurity can sometimes mask itself as arrogance. If the Star indicates the human as a link between the spirit and the outer world then the card reversed symbolizes the channels closed, and when the waters of life are dammed up inside, the outside can only become tired and depressed.

Figure 19

The Moon

The true task of the third line is not revelation but bringing that inner ecstasy back to consciousness. The Star contained no road back. It shows us dwelling in the glories of darkness transformed into light. To use that light we must pass through distortion and fear.

The Star experience lies beyond words or even form, though it implies forms emerging with the streams of water. In the Moon we see this process happening, as visions, myths and images. The Moon is the card of the imagination as it molds the energy of the Star into shapes that the consciousness can comprehend.

Myths are always distorted. They can never really say what they want, they can only appeal to things deep within the self. The Star stirred up the waters; as we return to outer awareness those waters give forth their creatures. Remember that the Star and the Sun give off their own light, but the Moon reflects the hidden light of the Sun. The imagination distorts because it is reflecting inner experience to the outer mind.

As the world's mythologies demonstrate the collective unconscious contains monsters as well as heros, fear as well as joy. This is one reason why we cover our sensitivity to life with the protective layer of ego consciousness, so we will no longer fear the dark and the distorting shadows of the Moon.

The Moon's eerie half-light has always brought out strange feelings in people and animals. One word for madness, 'lunacy', derives from 'luna', Latin for moon, and in the Middle Ages people believed that the souls of the insane had flown off to the moon. Today, too, many doctors and police have observed the prevalence of suicides and other signs of disturbed emotions during the full moon. Something about the moon excites fear and strangeness, just as the sun relaxes and consoles us. The Tarot Sun comes after the Moon; simplicity can only be appreciated after a journey through the lunar strangeness.

The dog and the wolf represent the 'animal self' roused by the Moon, just as a full moon can set both creatures howling all night long. The Emperor, directly above trump 18, showed us learning the rules of society so well that they become automatic. With the last line we go beyond this 'super ego' repression; in the process the 'id' wildness comes to the surface. A werewolf howling under a full moon is a vivid metaphor of the power of the unconscious to bring out something primitive and non-human in the most respectable people.

As 18 the Moon relates to 8. Strength saw the animal nature tamed, and channelled through the Hermit. Here no such direction is given; as we come back from the Star the beast returns in all its wildness. Only when the Star energy is fully integrated in the World will the animal self be wholly transformed. Notice that in Strength the woman, the human side, controls the lion. Even in the Devil the demons appear clearly human. But there are no people on trump 18. In that half-light our sense of ourselves as human breaks down.

We sense something of the Moon's wildness in the aftermath of a nightmare, when we feel strange within ourselves. The wild sensations are not the result of the nightmare; it is more the other way around. We said earlier that dreams are transformations of unconscious energy into images. A burst of energy which is too great for the dream mechanisms to peacefully assimilate can result in both a nightmare and the feeling when you wake up of the body being charged with wild energy.

Madness is also accompanied by uncontrolled sensations in the body. Very often lunacy takes the form of transformation into an animal. People will crawl on all fours, naked, howling at the moon. A sudden release of unconscious energy has disintegrated the personality. In the Tarot this very dangerous moment happens only after long preparation, with all the normal ego problems left behind. The shaman too experiences a transformation into a beast. Shamans will leap about and speak as animals during their trances. But the shaman, like the occultist, has prepared himself with years of preparation. He is also armed with the knowledge of what to expect, handed down from the generations of shamans who have gone before. Remember that the Moon's number adds up to 9, the Hermit. The teacher-guide of that card is not visible, for we must face the Moon alone, but the guidance given beforehand can help us find our way.

If the animals symbolize the savage in man, the crayfish is something very different. In one of his most vivid phrases Waite calls it 'that which lies deeper than the savage beast'. It symbolizes the most universal fears within the collective unconscious, experienced in visions as nameless demons. The emergence of such terrors is a well known occurrence to people who expose their lunar side through such methods as deep meditation or drugs. They are also seen as monsters encountered by shamans on their trance journeys. The arousal of these fears, often experienced as creatures emerging from water or pools of oily liquid, can produce unreasoning panic. Yet these images belong to our inner world; we cannot reach the Sun without passing them.

The crayfish half emerges from the water. Waite tells us it never comes completely onto land but always falls back again. The deepest errors are the ones that never fully take shape. We feel something inside, but we can never see just what it is. At the same time the half emerging crayfish suggests that in the journey back to consciousness the deep perceptions of the Star become distorted because we cannot bring it all back. For this reason too the Moon is disturbing, because the peace and wonder of the Star have become partially destroyed and lost.

And yet, despite the wildness, the fearful excitement, the cool light can calm as well. The Moon is said to increase on the 'side of mercy', a reference to the pillar of mercy on the Qabalistic Tree of Life. Even more striking, the drops of light falling on the animals' heads are, again, yods; the first letter of God's name and symbols of grace. If, through preparation and simple courage, we accept the wild things brought out by the deepest imagination, then the Moon brings peace, the terrors subside, and the imagination leads us back, enriched, with its wonders. Waite writes, 'Peace, be still; and there shall come a calm upon the waters.' The crayfish sinks back, the waters settle. The road remains.

The road leads through two towers, suggesting a gateway into unknown areas. The gateway is a very common symbol among mystics and shamans, seen also in many myths. Sometimes a circular pattern, like the mandala, or some physical formation, like a cave (very often compared to the vagina), the gateway allows us to leave the ordinary world to enter the strangeness of the mind.

The Tarot's two towers carry another meaning, as the last complete manifestation of that duality we first saw in the pillars of the High Priestess's temple. If the revelation of the Tower is not integrated with ordinary life then a new and more acute duality may result. At the same time, the very fact of having heard the speech of God totally changes our relation to the question of opposites. Previously duality was seen as basic to life, but we now know that in fact reality combines all things; where before the veil kept us from passing between the two pillars, here we have already passed through. We are looking at the two towers of consciousness from the other side. The task is not to pierce through to the inner truth but to take back that truth.

In divinatory readings the Moon indicates an excitement of the unconscious. We begin to experience strange emotions, dreams, fears, even hallucinations. If the card appears the right way up then the person will allow this to happen. When accepted, the imagination enriches life. But if the card appears reversed, it shows a struggle against the experience. This struggle leads to fear and often very disturbed emotions as the person does not allow the Moon's calming side to emerge.

Like the High Priestess the Moon indicates turning away from outer concerns and becoming introspective. It can indicate giving up some specific activity or simply a period of withdrawal. However, whilst the High Priestess symbolizes quiet intuition, the Moon is excited, stimulating images from the unconscious. Again, the Moon reversed signifies a disturbance. The person does not wish to turn away from the solar side, and may try to fight off the Moon by a great deal of activity. The Moon, however, will not be denied, and the fears can get stronger the more we fight it. The psyche, operating under its own laws for its own reasons, has turned to the Moon. If we allow ourselves to experience it the fears will turn to wonders and the gateways open to adventure.

(a)   *Figure 20*   *(b)*

The Sun

Like the Hanged Man above it the Sun is both a joyful release after the test shown in the previous card and a preparation for the death and rebirth in the two cards following. Justice required action as a response to the knowledge gained about ourselves. As a result the Hanged Man is passive. The Moon requires passive surrender, since there is no way we can control the visions rising under its influence. Therefore, the Sun shows an active, energized state. By accepting the Moon's fearful images we bring the energy outside ourselves, giving all of life a radiance.

Under the Sun everything becomes simple, joyous and physical. The light of the unconscious brought into daily life. The two children in the Oswald Wirth version, on the right, above the more common image for the trump, are sometimes called the eternal self and the mortal body. Holding hands, they have joined together. The two figures with the Sun above them returns us to the triangular motif first seen in the Hierophant two lines above. Here the joy and simplicity of the Sun does not mediate between the inner and outer poles of life but joins them together.

We are all children, in the way that sun religions speak of us all as holy children of our father, the sun. If you look at the bodies, in the picture, especially the female, you will see that they are adults. The

successful passage from the Tower has given them a childlike
simplicity.

The Tarot shows this passage in its various stages, giving the
impression of the passage of time. Sometimes, however, perhaps
most often, it happens all at once, the blinding revelation of the
Tower, the inner radiance of the Star, and the acute fear of the
Moon, all joined in a single instant of transformation. And the
aftermath is joy, a sense of all life and all the world being filled with
a wondrous light.

Among all people enlightenment bears the same characteristics,
whatever the cultural interpretation through mythology, doctrine,
psychological theory, etc. Enlightenment is an experience, not an
idea. The person feels struck by a burst of light, sometimes coloured,
like the yod drops in the Wirth card. Suddenly the world is seen or
felt, as spiritual and eternal, rather than the day to day existence of
drudgery and confusion. The person feels totally alive with a
childlike joy that, in fact, most children probably never know, for the
sunstruck person has gone beyond the child's fear of darkness by
travelling through it.

In its journey across the world the sun sees everything, and so
represents knowledge. Gods associated with the sun, like Apollo, are
said to know everything that happens. The sunstruck person feels a
sense of wisdom, of seeing everything with total clarity. He or she is
'lucid', a word which means clear and direct, but which literally
means 'filled with light'.

It is interesting that Apollo, god of light, was born from Leto,
goddess of night, and that his major shrine, the oracle at Delphi,
belonged originally to goddesses of darkness. Even under Apollo's
direction the wisdom and light of the oracle operated out of
darkness. It was Apollo who forced Oedipus to discover the mystery
within himself.

The spring sun brings forth life out of the dead winter ground. In
many places it was believed that the sun impregnates not only the
soil, but all women. When the biological means of reproduction was
discovered the role of the sun was not dropped but made more
subtle. People now saw the soul – the atman or true self – as sunlight
contained within the embryo. Buddhist myth states that Gautama,
in his mother's womb, was all light so that her belly shone like a
translucent screen over a powerful lamp. Zoroaster too blazed so
powerfully in his mother's womb that the neighbours ran with
buckets, thinking the house had caught fire.

The Gnostics carried this idea further, believing that the Fall had
broken up the godhead into the bits and pieces of existence. Most
important, the light had become imprisoned (rather than simply

contained) in individual bodies. It was each person's duty, through the Gnostic rites, to release the light within his body so that unity could be restored. The Qabalist Isaac Luria preached a similar doctrine. The Tree of Life, or Adam Kadmon, the unity of existence, had been shattered because the god light was too powerful for it. Again, the light became separated and imprisoned, so that it was the responsibility of each person to aid in 'tikkun', that is, restoration of the light to unity.

These doctrines derive from the Sun experience common to all cultures. The sunstruck person sees everything, each person, each animal, all the plants and rocks, even the very air, alive and holy, united through the light that fills all existence. And yet, the Sun is not the World. With trump 19 we perceive the universe as unified and alive. 21 embodies those feelings.

The usual drawing for the Sun shows the children within a garden, often standing in a circle. Douglas calls this the 'inner garden of the soul', a feeling of purity and holiness, a new Garden of Eden. When we liberate and transform the energy locked inside us we find that the Garden of Eden was never really lost, but has always existed within us.

The Rider pack shows its single child riding out of a garden. For Waite the Sun experience was essentially a burst of freedom. It was a breaking loose, a wonderful liberation from ordinary restricted consciousness to openness and freedom.

The grey, stone wall in the picture represents the past life, bound by a narrow perception of reality. The super-consciousness of the Sun is characterized by feeling a part of the whole world rather than an isolated individual. We can perhaps combine the two images for the trump by saying that once you realize that the Garden of Eden exists within you, you are free to leave it, taking it with you always as you create a new life.

The number 19 suggests a higher level of 9. The light contained in the Hermit's lantern, the wisdom of his teachings, here bursts forth as Abulafia's ecstatic third level of Qabalah. We said of the Hermit that the old man and the bleak mountain were illusions required because the inner self could only be reached through withdrawal. Here the truth has emerged and the robed stiff Hermit is transformed into a gloriously open child. The other half of 19 is 1. The Magician force joined to the Hermit wisdom is super-consciousness. The energy of life united with its meaning and purpose.

1 plus 9 equals 10, the Wheel of Fortune whose vision was of something outside us that we tried to comprehend. Here we see life in a visionary way from inside ourselves. And in this kind of vision

there are no mysteries and no symbols, only the universe, filled with light.

The Sun's divinatory meanings are as simple and direct as the wondrous children in the pictures. The card signifies joy, happiness, and a great sense of the beauty of life. In its deepest sense it means looking at the world in a wholly new way, seeing all life united in joy and light. Above all it is a card of optimism, energy and wonder.

Reversed, the good things do not become lost but confused, as if the sun had become clouded over. Life is still giving the person a time of simple happiness, but it cannot be seen so clearly. The person is no longer lucid and must work to realize the joy which is the great gift of the Sun.

Figure 21

Judgement
Under the Sun we see all of life as filled with spiritual light. This awareness of eternal truth frees us from all illusion and fear so that now we feel, like a call from deep inside, the urge to dissolve ourselves completely into the spirit and wondrous life contained in every being.

This call comes from both inside and outside us, for one of the effects of the Sun was to break down the artificial barrier between inner experience and the outer world. We feel the call in our deepest selves as if the very cells of the body were filled with a shout of joy.

At the same time, we recognize that the call comes from some force greater than any individual life.

This idea of Judgement as a call to rise to a more meaningful existence has its analogues in more ordinary situations. Sometimes in life a person can come to a crossroads (notice the cross in the banner) where a decision is required on whether to make some great change. And sometimes it can seem as if something within the person has already decided and the only choice left to the conscious self is to follow with the appropriate action. The old ways of believing and thinking, the old situations, have died without ourselves even noticing.

Most versions of the trump show only the angel and the figures rising up. The Rider pack adds a range of mountains in the background. Waite calls them the 'mountains of abstract thought'. The term implies eternal truth beyond the limited knowledge available to us through ordinary means.

One of the basic features of morality is the inability to know anything in an absolute sense. We are bound by our short lives and by the fact that all knowledge comes to our minds through the medium of the senses. In modern physics we learn that scientific investigation can never form an exact picture of reality because the observer is always a part of the universe that he or she is observing. In the same way, each person's thoughts about and perceptions of life are influenced by that person's past experience. 'Abstract thought' implies, like the Platonic ideals, a sense of the absolute.

We reach this 'abstraction' by making one last descent into the waters of nothingness in order to rise up liberated from all partial knowledge. Death, directly above, showed a dissolution. There the ego was dying and the trump emphasized the fear of letting go. Here all illusions of isolation are dissolved, and the emphasis rests not on the death but on the resurrection.

We call the card Judgement because, like Justice, it involves coming to terms with past experience as a part of going beyond it. With Justice the experience and the response were personal, based on your actions in the past. Here a force greater than yourself is leading and calling you, and the Judgement is not simply on the meaning of your own life but on the true nature of existence, and the way in which you and all beings are a part of it.

At times in this book we have referred to the Hebrew letters assigned to the different trumps. Usually we have followed the system in which the Fool is Aleph. There is another system, where the Magician receives Aleph, and in that system Judgement bears the letter Resh. Resh means 'head' and refers, like Waite's mountains, to the true mind awakened by the call. Resh also suggests Rosh Hashanah, the Jewish New Year, literally 'head of the year'. Now, Rosh Hashanah is not the start of the calendar, like the secular New Year, but represents, in fact, the anniversary of creation. Similarly, Judgement indicates not a change of circumstances but a new consciousness, one directly acquainted with the truth through a merging of yourself with the forces of life.

The Wheel of Fortune, with its invisible laws of psychic cause and effect, was 10; Judgement is 20, 10 multiplied by 2. Through the workings of the last line we reveal the High Priestess's hidden wisdom so that now we understand the inner mysteries concealed in the Wheel.

The cross in the banner indicates a meeting of opposites, a joining of all the things that had been separated. It symbolizes a meeting of two kinds of time; the ordinary time we perceive with our senses and by which we live from day to day, and eternity, the spiritual perception of life. These two times are symbolized by the horizontal and vertical lines of the cross. Their meeting in the centre indicates that the higher self does not abandon its old activities but goes about them in a new way.

The card above Judgement is the Lovers and, in the Rider pack, also shows an angel. There, however, the angel was a glimpse of a greater truth experienced through the medium of love. Here the angel leans down from the cloud to call to us. In the traditional version of the Sun we saw the final example of that triangular motif begun in trumps 5 and 6. Here we see a child between the two people. The poles of life have come together to form a new reality, in the way that every child is both a combination of its parents and something completely new.

The child in front stands with his back to us. The new existence is a mystery, with no way for us to know what it will be like until we experience it. The child's hidden face also implies that we do not really know ourselves, and that we cannot until we hear and respond to the call. Virtually all mythologies contain stories of the hero separated from his parents and raised as an ordinary child, with other people, and very often the child himself, knowing nothing of his true identity. King Arthur, Moses, Theseus, and Christ all follow this pattern. We see this same idea in many science fiction stories, where the hero awakes in a strange place with no memory; his search for his true identity leads him to discover great powers within himself. Very often he finds himself in the centre of either a powerful plot or at the very workings of nature. We have all 'forgotten' our true identities and have become separated from our 'parents'. And when we find or create our true selves, we will find ourselves at the centre of the universe. For the centre is everywhere.

Most decks show only the three people in the foreground. Waite's addition of three more people, all facing us, suggests that while Judgement leads to the unknown, there is still an awareness (also symbolized as well by the mountains) of the ways in which the unknown life will develop.

The extra people imply another, very vital point. By showing a whole group rising the trump reminds us that there is no personal liberation. Each human being is part of the human race and therefore responsible for the development of the race as a whole. No one can be truly free while someone else is enslaved. Buddha was said to have come back as a boddhisatva because he understood that he could not liberate himself until he had liberated all humanity. At the same time, any single liberation liberates everybody. This is because any person's attainment of Judgement and the World alter the circumstances of everybody's life. Gautama's Buddhahood and the resurrection of Christ are seen as events that have totally changed the world.

In the divinatory readings the card of Judgement carries a special significance. Whatever else is going on around you, there is a push, a call from within, to make some important change. The change can refer to something mundane and immediate, or to an entire shift in the way a person looks at life – depending on the other cards, and the subject of the reading. The important thing is the call. In effect, the person has already changed; the old situations, the old self, have already died. It is simply a matter of recognizing it.

Judgement reversed can indicate that the person wishes to answer the call but does not know what to do. More often it shows someone trying to deny the call, usually from a fear of the unknown. There may, in fact, be a great many rational reasons why the person should not follow the suggested change: lack of money, lack of preparation or responsibilities. Judgement, the right way up or reversed, indicates that all the objections are excuses. When the card is upside down the excuses become dominant; the person remains standing in the grave. The word Judgement implies that the reality of life has changed. The only choice is to follow.

Figure 22

The World

What can we say of an understanding, a freedom and rapture beyond words? The unconscious known consciously, the outer self unified with the forces of life, knowledge that is not knowledge at all but a constant ecstatic dance of being – they are all true and yet not true.

We have already observed a great deal about this card and its images. The number as well as the two wands unify the Magician and the High Priestess. We saw the World foreshadowed as well in the Wheel of Fortune, and reflected how the symbols of that trump are now living realities. One way or another, the Wheel has come up for virtually every card in the last line. The purpose of this line can be described as that of uniting ourselves with all those things seen in trump 10 as external vision, that is, fate, the workings of life, the elements of existence. When the unity is achieved the symbols vanish, dissolved into a dancing spirit.

We saw the World in the Hanged Man, by number and picture. Trump 12 maintained its bliss through complete inactivity. But even the World Tree is an illusion created by the mind's need to grasp onto something. When we have dissolved our isolated selves into that water lying beneath the Hanged Man's glowing face we learn that true unity lies in movement.

Everything in the universe moves, the Earth around the sun, the sun within the galaxy, the galaxies in clusters, all cycling around each other. There is no centre, no place where we can say, 'Here it all began, here it all stops.' Yet the centre exists, everywhere, for in a dance the dancer does not move around any arbitrary point in space, but rather the dance carries its own sense of unity focused around a constantly moving, constantly peaceful centre. Nothing and everything all at once.

And so we return to the Fool. Innocence and emptiness, united with wisdom. As we said at the beginning, of all the Major Arcana cards, only these two are moving. The oval wreath suggests the number 0, with all its symbolism. It implies as well the cosmic egg, the archetype of emergence; all things exist in potential and all potentials are realized. The self is everywhere in all things. The sashes at the top and bottom of the wreath are tied into infinity signs, indicating that the self is not enclosed but open to the universe.

The sashes are red, the colour of the root chakra in Kundalini symbolism. The dancer has not lost her physical being, her root in material, sexual reality. Instead, the energy is constantly flowing, transformed and renewed. The green of the wreath symbolizes the natural world raised up rather than abandoned. Green is also the colour of love and healing, radiating wholeness to everyone, even those who are not consciously aware of it. Purple (the banner) is the colour of divinity and blue (the sky) the colour of communication. When we know that divinity is not something out there, but within ourselves, then our very presence communicates this truth to those around us.

One of the World's analogues is Shiva, Lord of the Cosmic Dance. He too dances with the arms out, one foot down and the other raised, the head balanced and the expression calm. The right foot of both figures is 'planted' in the physical world, while the raised left leg symbolizes the soul's release. When we become most joined to life, at that moment we realize our freedom. The face is neither sad nor joyful but at peace, free in its emptiness. The arms are open to all experience.

Dancing Shiva is usually depicted as an hermaphrodite, one half of the body Shiva, the other Parvati, his female side. The World dancer is also hermaphroditic, the dual sexual organs concealed by the banner, as if to say that the unity they represent lies beyond our knowing. In discussing the Lovers we referred to the widespread belief that all people were originally hermaphrodites. The dancer expresses and unites all the different sides of being.

The same feeling that leads us to a 'memory' of primeval

hermaphroditism has taken people a step further to the image of the entire universe having once been a single human being. We find this belief among the Gnostics, in Blake, in German, Indian, and other mythologies, and in great detail in the Qabalah. There the figure bears the name 'Adam Kadmon' and is said to be the original creation emanating from the unknowable God. Rather than a physical being, Adam Kadmon, also hermpahroditic, was described as pure light. Only when the figure broke up into the separate parts of the universe did the light become 'imprisoned' in matter. It is a fascinating fact that the contemporary scientific theories of cosmogony describe the universe as originally one particle. At the moment that the particle broke up it was all pure light; only later, as the pieces became more isolated did some of that energy condense into matter, following Einstein's famous formulation, $E=mc^2$.

The myths consider the break-up of primeval Man an irreversible event. Occultists, however, believe in the possibility of restoration. By following the process outlined in the Major Arcana we become united with life and so ourselves become Adam Kadmon and Shiva-Parvati.

Adam Kadmon is linked to the Tree of Life, with its ten sephiroth, or points of emanation. We have already seen the connection between this figure and the Tarot through the Tree's 22 paths. The World Dancer, by her posture, is an exact representation of the Tree of Life's most common form. The Tree is drawn in the following way:

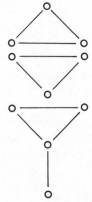

Very simplified, the top triangle is super-consciousness, the middle is consciousness, the bottom the unconscious, and the final point, the root of the Tree, is the manifestation of all these principles in the physical world.

In the Dancer the top triangle is the crown of the head and the points of the shoulders, the middle triangle is the hands and the genitals, the bottom triangle is the crossed leg and right foot. At the same time it is all one body. By contemplating the dancer we learn that the unconscious, conscious and super-conscious are not separate parts or even separate stages of being, but are all one. But what about the tenth sephira, the root of the Tree? We find it not in the body but in all the universe, the wonderful ground of being in which we move.

Descriptions, metaphors, even contemplation can only hint at the wonders embodied in trump 21. When the card comes up in divination these wonders become further reduced to the ordinary situations with which most readings concern themselves. The card means success, achievement, satisfaction. To greater or lesser degree it indicates a unification of the person's inner sense of being with his or her outer activities.

Reversed, the trump indicates stagnation, the movement and growth slowed down to the point of being stopped. Or so it seems. In fact, the freedom and rapture of the World exist always in potential, to be released when the person feels ready to begin, once more, the dance of life.

These are the meanings of the World in divination. Its true meanings are unknowable. They are a goal, a hope, an intuition. The way to that goal, the steps and music of the dance, lies in the living images of the Major Arcana.

Bibliography

Butler, Bill, *The Definitive Tarot* (Rider and Company, London, 1975)

Case, Paul Foster, *The Tarot, A Key to the Wisdom of the Ages* (Macoy Publishing Company, Richmond, Virginia, 1947)

Crowley, Aleister, *The Book of Thoth* (Samuel Weiser, New York, 1944)*

D'Agostino, Joseph, *Tarot: The Royal Path to Wisdom* (Samuel Weiser, New York, 1976)*

Douglas, Alfred, *The Tarot* (Penguin, London, 1972)

Eliade, Mircea, *Shamanism* (Princeton University Press, Princeton, 1964)

Gray, Eden, *The Tarot Revealed* (Bantam, New York, 1969)

Haich, Elizabeth, *Wisdom of the Tarot* (New York, 1975)

Kaplan, Stuart, *The Encyclopedia of Tarot* (U.S. Games, Limited, 1978)*

Malory, Thomas, *Work*, ed. Eugene Vinaver (Oxford, London, 1959)

Scholem, Gershon, *Major Trends in Jewish Mysticism* (Shocken, New York, 1941)

Scholem, Gershon, *On the Kabbalah and its Symbolism* (Shocken, New York, 1965)

Waite, Arthur Edward, *The Pictorial Key to the Tarot* (University Books, New York, 1910, 1959). All quotations from Waite are taken from this book.

Wang, Robert, *An Introduction to the Golden Dawn Tarot* (Aquarian Press, Wellingborough, 1978)

Williams, Charles, *The Greater Trumps* (Victor Gollancz, London, 1932)

*U.K. Distributors: Thorsons Publishers Limited, Wellingborough, Northamptonshire.